Careers for You Series

## CAREERS FOR

# KIDS AT HEART

## & Others Who Adore Children

**MARJORIE EBERTS**
**MARGARET GISLER**

THIRD EDITION

**McGraw·Hill**

New York   Chicago   San Francisco   Lisbon   London   Madrid   Mexico City
Milan   New Delhi   San Juan   Seoul   Singapore   Sydney   Toronto

**Library of Congress Cataloging-in-Publication Data**

Eberts, Marjorie.
    Careers for kids at heart & others who adore children / by Marjorie Eberts,
Margaret Gisler. — 3rd ed.
       p.  cm.  —  (McGraw-Hill careers for you series)
      ISBN 0-07-145880-8 (alk. paper)
       1.  Child care—Vocational guidance—United States.   I. Gisler, Margaret.
II. Eberts, Marjorie. Careers for kids at heart & others who adore children.
III. Title.

HQ778.63.E374 2006
362.7'12'02373—dc22                                 2005017562

* * * * * * * * * * * * * * * * * * * * * * * * * * * * * * * * * * * * *

*To all the kids at heart and others
who adore children and who have
enhanced the lives of children through
their work, and especially to Pennie
Needham, whose teaching and tutoring
careers have been devoted to helping
all children succeed in school*

1  2  3  4  5  6  7  8  9  0   DOC/DOC   0  9  8  7  6

ISBN 0-07-145880-8

McGraw-Hill books are available at special quantity discounts to use as premiums and
sales promotions, or for use in corporate training programs. For more information,
please write to the Director of Special Sales, Professional Publishing, McGraw-Hill,
Two Penn Plaza, New York, NY 10121-2298. Or contact your local bookstore.

This book is printed on acid-free paper.

# Contents

# CHAPTER ONE

# Careers for Kids at Heart and Others Who Adore Children

*It takes a village to raise a child.*
—African proverb

Parents depend upon the loving care of kids at heart and others who adore children to aid them in the demanding task of raising their children. Perhaps this is even more true today than it has been in the past in this country as working mothers now greatly outnumber stay-at-home moms. Parents have always shared the task of raising children with teachers and health providers. Now working parents need the help of workers at child care centers, at-home care providers, nannies, and babysitters. And all parents are interested in having helpers provide their children with enjoyable opportunities to participate in sport, recreational, art, and entertainment activities. The climate is perfect for kids at heart to find satisfying careers that will let them play an important role in the lives of children.

Japan devotes one day a year to children on Children's Day. Choose a career that lets you work with children and every day will be Children's Day for you. Working with children is not only an important career in our culture, it is also a very satisfying one. Children idolize their teachers, scout leaders, karate instructors, and youth ministers. They show great affection with frequent smiles, hugs, and kisses for their nannies, babysitters, and child care providers. Your praise is like sunshine to them. Working with children on a day-to-day basis is not just rewarding, it is also an awesome responsibility, for you are shaping the kind of adults they will become. You are teaching children basic values as they learn from you to respect other people and property. Furthermore, whenever you are with children, you are a role model demonstrating how to handle people and situations. Children will imitate your actions, so you must constantly be aware of the example you are setting for them.

## Do You Really Want to Work with Children?

Are you truly the type of person who wants to spend eight hours a day working with children? If you can answer yes to most of the following questions, then you are truly a kid at heart or someone who adores children and should investigate a career working with children.

1. Do you take satisfaction in helping children acquire new skills?
2. Have you enjoyed being a babysitter, assistant scout leader, or coach of a children's sports team?
3. Do you take pleasure in talking to children?
4. Do you like to participate in activities with children?
5. Are you an avid listener when you have conversations with children?
6. Have you thought about what it would be like to have a career working with children?

7. Do you enjoy encouraging children to use their imaginations?
8. Are you patient with children even when they misbehave?

## An Amazing Variety of Careers

When you consider a career working with children, an astounding number of possibilities emerge. And just as you have a choice of jobs, you also have a choice of working with a wide range of ages. You may prefer a particular age group, such as newborns, toddlers, preschoolers, elementary schoolchildren, or older children in junior high or middle school. Or you can elect to work with children of all ages.

Glance through the following list to explore just a few of the career opportunities that exist for those who want to work with children.

art teacher
au pair
babysitter
camp counselor or director
child care worker
child psychologist or psychiatrist
children's photographer
clown
counselor
dance teacher
family restaurant employee
juvenile court judge
librarian
magician
music teacher
nanny
pediatrician
pediatric dentist
pediatric nurse or nurse practitioner
police officer in the juvenile division
preschool teacher
radio, television, or theatrical performer
recreation worker
social worker
speech therapist
sports instructor
teacher
tutor

This book is designed to help all those who are kids at heart and who adore children to realize their aspirations of finding jobs that will let them work with children. Here is a brief overview of some of the jobs you will read about.

## Child Care Center Careers

The good news is that job openings at child care centers are plentiful. The bad news is that these jobs typically provide low wages and few benefits. You can work for nonprofit organizations such as religious institutions, community agencies, school systems, and state and local governments. There are also jobs at centers that are run for profit. Some of these are associated with local or national chains. The possibility of working for a business also exists as more businesses are opening child care centers for their employees. No matter where you work, you have the joy of sharing your life with children and receiving their affection.

## At-Home Child Care Careers

Imagine never having to think about leaving home to do your job and at the same time being able to take care of children full-time. This can happen if you elect to establish a child care facility in your own home. You will, however, be running a business, which involves acquiring the necessary licenses, obtaining insurance, buying supplies, advertising your services, and hiring others to help you. You also have the responsibility of setting up a program that helps each child develop socially, emotionally, physically, and mentally.

## Nanny Careers

Movie stars, corporate executives, and just ordinary people hire nannies to take care of their young children. So many families want nannies that the demand is far greater than the supply. Here is a job that often involves twenty-four-hour care of one or more children within the family home. You will plan the children's days and supervise most of their activities, which include such tasks as bathing, comforting, reading to, disciplining, preparing meals for, and playing with the children. But most of all you will give them the love and guidance young children need.

## Babysitting Careers

More than one million people in this country have chosen babysitting as a career. Parents of young children need babysitters when they want to go out for an evening or on a vacation. Working parents need sitters to care for children after school or in the summer. A few babysitters watch the same children every day, but most sitters supervise different children on a part-time or irregular basis.

## Teaching Careers

Young children just love to learn. And they also love their teachers. You can choose to work with very young children in nursery school or Head Start programs. Or you can work as a kindergarten teacher preparing children for elementary school. In the first three grades of elementary school, you will be teaching children basic skills, while in later grades you will expand these skills and teach content-area subjects such as history, health, geography, and English. Of course, you don't have to be a teacher to work in a school. Schools also need secretaries, librarians, bus drivers, maintenance workers, and cooks.

## Sports and Recreation Careers

Children are enthusiastic and energetic, and they love sports and all forms of recreation. Some want to become more skilled in a particular area. Others want to investigate new recreational opportunities. Whether your expertise is camping or karate, there are children who want to learn more about it. The special dividend to careers in sports and recreation is that you and the children will have a great time together.

## Children's Health Careers

Children need expert help when they are sick and require skilled care so that they will remain healthy. Being a health care professional is a perfect job for compassionate people who enjoy working with children. Jobs in pediatrics almost always require special training and licensing. Certain jobs, such as pediatric physician or cardiologist, require years of postgraduate training. Your workplace will usually be at a health care facility such as a hospital, clinic, or doctor's office. Wherever you work, your coworkers will share your interest in helping children. Many times you will work together as a team.

## Child Welfare Careers

In today's world, not all children live in perfect or even very good environments. Many children live in situations where their basic needs are not met. Some children don't even have homes. Unfortunately, there are also children who are abused by their parents, other family members, or strangers. Some children do not attend school regularly; others may commit crimes. As a social worker, police officer, juvenile court judge, court referee, or child advocate, you can have a career helping troubled children and their families. All of these jobs will let you make a real difference in children's lives.

## Arts and Entertainment Careers

The world of arts and entertainment can bring a new dimension to children's lives and expand their horizons. What could be more rewarding than helping children explore art, music, dance, or theater? Or would you prefer to be an entertainer and use your skills to amuse children, as clowns and magicians do?

## More Careers Focusing on Children

Wherever you find children, there will be jobs that let you interact with them in some way. Be a children's librarian, and you can help children select books. Be a children's photographer, and you can spend time posing them to get the perfect picture for the family album. Be an author of children's books, and you may be as beloved by children as Dr. Seuss was.

## Exploring Your Interests

As you have discovered so far in this book, you can work with children in many different jobs. Take the following quiz to help you define which areas are most appealing:

1. Would you prefer to work with a specific age group, such as newborns, toddlers, preschoolers, or school-age children?
2. Do you see yourself working with one child, a few children, or a group of children?
3. Do you want to work with both children and their families?
4. Do you want to work directly with children or just be involved in activities dealing with children?
5. Are you most interested in a job involved in child care, education, health care, welfare, or recreation?
6. Would you like a job that involves supervising other employees?
7. Would you prefer to work for a small or large organization?
8. Do you want to work in the private or public sector?
9. Would you prefer to work alone or with others?
10. Do you want to own and operate your own business?

## Job Qualifications

Organizations will not hire you just because you adore children and want to work with them. This is not a sufficient qualification; more is required for almost every job that involves the care of children. Even child care workers who have jobs that pay the minimum wage need to have some formal training in most states. Furthermore, most jobs involving the education, health, or welfare of children require at least a bachelor's degree.

Besides formal training, you must have energy and enthusiasm to work successfully with children. For most jobs, you will also need to demonstrate an ability to communicate effectively with children as well as with their parents. Furthermore, you should be a role model that parents will want their children to emulate.

Many organizations prefer to hire people who have work experience. This could be your biggest challenge in landing your first job. Fortunately, such activities as being an assistant scout leader, babysitting, coaching a team, or volunteering as a tutor are usually considered a satisfactory substitute for paid work experience. You can get a head start on your career by becoming involved in these activities while you are in high school.

## Where the Jobs Are

For kids at heart and others who adore children, jobs can be found wherever there are children. In most communities, even the smallest ones, you will be able to find a job as a babysitter, child care worker, or teacher. However, if you want to teach tennis to children, photograph children exclusively, or be a pediatrician, you will need to live in or near a larger city. You can expect to find the greatest number of jobs working with children in major metropolitan areas where demand is likely higher for child psychiatrists, karate instructors, and child advocates.

## Finding a Job

Studying newspaper ads in papers and online, directly contacting organizations, using an employment agency, and talking to friends are all effective ways to find jobs. Becoming familiar with professional organizations and the services they offer can also be a successful job-seeking strategy. The Appendix provides a list of the names, addresses, and websites of some of these organizations. Frequently, these organizations publish journals or newsletters that list job openings. And some organizations even hold job fairs where employers come to actively seek new employees. You can also use the Internet to research association websites and job bulletin boards.

## Making a Difference in Others' Lives

Many people work at jobs that they consider very satisfying and rewarding. They like what they do in the workplace and enjoy going to work every day. Furthermore, they take pride in their work. If you truly adore children, a job working with children will bring you all the previously mentioned satisfactions. It will also let you make a difference in the lives of others. By your actions on the job, you will be able to help children get a solid start on their futures. Well-trained teachers can successfully impart skills and help children develop a love of learning. Loving caregivers in child care centers can help young children develop confidence in their fledgling abilities. Devoted nannies can fill children's early years with love. Social workers can find excellent foster homes for abused children. No matter what your job working with children is, you will have the opportunity to make a positive impact on their young lives.

# CHAPTER TWO

# Child Care Center Careers

*Definition: A child care center is a facility, other than a private residence, where child care is provided by a paid staff of caregivers for one or more children.*

oday's parents rely on child care providers to allow them to go to work. No longer are most American mothers staying home with their children. The stay-at-home moms shown in early television shows have become a definite minority. Today, approximately 65 percent of all moms with children between birth and age five are working outside their homes. And this number is expected to increase by the year 2010, when the number of women in the workforce will exceed the number of working men. This is good news for everyone who wants to work in child care, as there now is a tremendous demand for qualified personnel. Because the wages for child care workers are so low, the annual turnover rate is a very high 31 percent, adding to the demand for workers.

As it has become the rule rather than the exception for mothers to work outside the home, a variety of child care options has emerged. The most popular of these options is the child care center, with more than 31 percent of all children between birth and five years of age in center-based programs. There are now more than 115,000 centers in the United States serving preschoolers and school-age children in before- and after-school programs.

Another important option, at-home family day care, is discussed in Chapter 3, while in-home care by nannies and babysitters is discussed in Chapters 4 and 5.

## A Brief History of Child Care Centers

Child care centers are not new. They have existed for more than two hundred years. The centers originated in England and Scotland when women left their homes to work in the first factories. Since the women could neither leave their children at home nor have them at their sides while they worked, factory owners established rooms for the children that were supervised by untrained adults and older children. It was not until one hundred years later that child care centers were established in the United States, when manufacturing became a major industry and women joined the workforce.

The number of child care centers in this country increased during World War II as the government provided funds to set up centers at defense plants for working mothers. After the war, these centers were shut down, and many women left the workforce. The number of child care centers increased dramatically during the 1960s, when women started returning to the workforce. Then in the 1980s the number really multiplied as more and more mothers with children started working outside their homes. It is projected that the number of child care centers will continue to increase through 2010.

### A Closer Look at Child Care Centers

Child care centers provide care in a large group situation, usually divided by age or developmental level. As the number of child care centers has grown, so has the diversity of services they offer. At first these centers were thought of as an organized continuation of babysitting. But as time went on, parents wanted their children to have solid developmental and educational experiences as well as basic care. They also wanted expanded operating hours so they could drop their children off before work and pick them up after work. Then the need arose for parents to have before- and after-school care and summer programs for their school-age children. And as mothers began rejoining the workforce almost immediately after childbirth, they demanded care for infants as well as toddlers and preschoolers.

The diverse needs of parents have resulted in a variety of child care centers that range from offering a complete array of services to just a few services or one specific service. You can find centers that run from six in the morning until seven in the evening and have programs for infants, toddlers, preschoolers, and school-age children. There are also centers devoted solely to the care of infants, while others cater to ages two, three, and four.

Child care centers vary in size from those caring for a few children to those caring for several hundred. Roughly 47 percent of all child care worker jobs are located in centers with fewer than twenty employees. Nearly all centers have fewer than fifty workers as is shown in Table 1 and Figure 1.

**TABLE 1. Percentage of Child Care Workers Employed by Establishment Size**

|                    | 1 TO 4 | 5 TO 19 | 20 TO 49 | 50 OR MORE |
| ------------------ | ------ | ------- | -------- | ---------- |
| **Establishments** | 39%    | 44%     | 15%      | 2%         |
| **Employment**     | 6%     | 41%     | 37%      | 17%        |

Source: U.S. Department of Labor, Bureau of Labor Statistics

Child care centers operate under a wide variety of ownerships. There are both nonprofit centers and centers operated for profit. More than half are nonprofit centers operated by religious groups, community agencies, public schools, hospitals, colleges, and

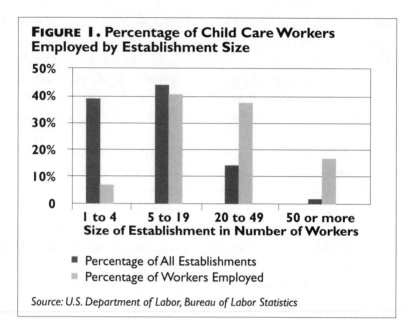

**FIGURE 1.** Percentage of Child Care Workers Employed by Establishment Size

Percentage of All Establishments
Percentage of Workers Employed

Source: U.S. Department of Labor, Bureau of Labor Statistics

universities. About one-fourth of the for-profit establishments are operated by large chains. You can find child care centers in shopping centers, churches, school buildings, office buildings, and neighborhoods. The most successful centers are found in locations where it is easy for parents to drop off and pick up their children on the way to and from work.

## Opportunities in Child Care Centers

Not too long ago, job seekers who wanted to work in child care centers had a limited number of choices. Today, qualified job seekers can usually choose the type of program that appeals to them. They can also decide whether they want to work at a center run by a church, a business, a chain, a public school, an individual, or a wide variety of organizations.

With so many thousands of centers throughout the country, job seekers can generally choose where they want to work and may even be able to find a job just a few minutes from their homes. In addition, child care center workers often have the opportunity to work either full-time or part-time and to select what hours they will work. Of course, the greatest number of options will be found in large cities. For example, if you live in Philadelphia, Atlanta, Indianapolis, or San Jose and want a job close to home with a chain teaching toddlers, you can probably find one. Because of the overwhelming demand for child care center workers, it is easy to find jobs tailored to your specifications.

The job titles in child care centers vary. Also, the type and number of positions depend greatly on the size of a center. At a very large child care center, you will probably find the following positions on the career ladder:

- Director
- Assistant director
- Head teacher
- Lead teacher
- Teacher
- Assistant teacher (aide)

Large centers also employ office managers, clerical staff, cooks, van drivers, and maintenance workers.

## Aptitudes Needed for Working at a Child Care Center

If you are a kid at heart or someone who truly adores children, you may be seriously thinking of a career in some capacity at a child care center. Being fascinated by children, however, is not sufficient reason to assume that you have the necessary aptitudes and skills. The following list outlines the major qualifications needed for a successful career at a child care center:

- knowledge of child development and child-rearing practices
- nurturing skills
- an abiding affection for children
- high energy level
- good health
- sensitivity to the feelings of children
- the ability to handle emergency situations
- excellent communication skills with both children and adults
- dependability
- willingness to keep abreast of the latest child development and education information
- an abundance of patience
- willingness to spend the workday primarily in the company of children
- solid organizational skills
- tolerance of the clutter that surrounds young children and of their tendency to be messy
- a calm disposition

You will not generally be working alone at a child care center no matter what your job is. Directors work with assistant directors and teachers, and teachers must work with other teachers, assistant teachers, and supervisors.

Answer the following questions to see whether you possess the skills to relate well to other staff members:

1. Are you willing to listen to others' suggestions and ideas?
2. Are you able to accept criticism?
3. Do you have the confidence to ask for help when you need it?

4. Do you have the ability to be a team player?
5. Are you willing to share your own ideas with others?
6. Are you fast to express support of coworkers?
7. Are you slow to criticize coworkers?

## Employment Requirements for Jobs in Child Care Centers

Most states now have legislation that requires the staff (teachers and directors) at child care centers to have some training in early childhood education. Quite often you will need to have a Child Development Associate (CDA) credential, which is offered by the Council for Early Childhood Professional Recognition. As part of obtaining the CDA credential, you may take course work at a local school or college to learn the skills needed to work in a child care center. The CDA credential is further discussed in Chapter 6. There are very few states that do not require any training or experience in order to be a teacher in a public child care center. You can find out about each state's licensing requirements for teachers and master teachers from:

National Child Care Information Center
10530 Rosehaven Street, Suite 400
Fairfax, VA 22030
www.nccic.org

If you live in a state like California, considerable course work in early childhood education is required for both public and private centers. On the other hand, you can find a job as an aide in most states in both public and private centers with a high school diploma and little or no experience. As an example, study the following employment requirements to see exactly what training you would need to get a job in a California child care center. Note that more training is required for public centers than for private centers.

## Private Centers in California

**Aide.** Aides must be at least eighteen years old, high school graduates, and under the supervision of a qualified teacher at all times.

**Teacher.** The state requires teachers in private centers to complete a minimum of twelve units at the college level of early childhood education courses in the following areas:

1. Child Development/Psychology (three units)
2. Child, Family, and Community (three units)
3. Curriculum (six units)

Some private centers may hire individuals as teachers after they have completed six units of early childhood education courses, provided that they are currently enrolled in a further six units.

**Director.** Directors must have the twelve units of early childhood education required for teachers, three units in administration, and four years of experience in a licensed center. Individuals with an A.A. degree in early childhood education need two years of experience in a licensed center plus three units in administration, and those with a B.A. in early childhood education need a children's center supervisory permit or one year of experience in a licensed center in administration.

Additional classes in safety and health, such as CPR and first aid, may be needed to work at a center. Also, the requirements to work at a center for school-age children are slightly different.

## Public Centers in California

A Child Development Permit is required to work in state-funded early child care and development programs. There are six levels of permits that include the education and experience requirements in Table 2.

**TABLE 2.** Education and Experience Requirements for Child Care Workers

| TITLE | EDUCATION REQUIREMENT | EXPERIENCE REQUIREMENT |
|---|---|---|
| Assistant | 6 units Early Childhood Education (ECE) or Child Development (CD) | None |
| Associate Teacher | 12 units ECE/CD (including core courses) | 50 days of 3+ hours per day within 2 years |
| Teacher | 24 units ECE/CD (including core courses) + 16 General Education (GE) units | 175 day of 3+ hours per day within 4 years |
| Master Teacher | 24 units ECE/CD (including core courses) + 16 GE units + 6 specialization units + 2 adult supervision units | 350 days of 3+ hours per day within 4 years |
| Site Supervisor | A.A. (or 60 units) with 24 ECE/CD units (including core courses) + 6 units administration + 2 units adult supervision | 350 days of 3+ hours per day within 4 years, including at least 100 days of supervising adults |
| Program Director | B.A. (or 126 units) with 24 ECE/CD units (including core courses) + 6 units administration + 2 units adult supervision | Site supervisor status and one program year of site supervisor experience |

Source: State of California

# On the Job in Child Care Centers

## The Setting

It's a small world everywhere in a child care center. Chairs and tables are just the right size for the children who use them. And each classroom is divided into intriguing areas that lure children into participating in different activities. You will find some or all of these areas in a typical classroom:

| | |
|---|---|
| art | manipulatives |
| blocks | mathematics |
| books | music |
| computer | puzzles |
| dress-up | science |
| fitness | self-help toys |
| housekeeping | weather |

This is your workday world when you choose a career working at a child care center.

## The Staff

In the classroom, teachers work together closely. A classroom may have a head teacher, lead teacher, several teachers, assistant teachers (sometimes called aides), and volunteers. A head teacher has more administrative functions, while the lead teacher is next in command in a classroom that has both teaching positions. Teachers' titles and duties vary from school to school. The number of teachers within a classroom depends on how many children are in the room. Many states have established ratios that spell out how many children a teacher can handle. Some also regulate how many children of a certain age can be in a group. No matter where you work, you will always work with a small group of children.

Table 3 shows California regulations for the appropriate teacher-child ratio in private child care centers.

**TABLE 3.** Teacher-Child Ratio in California

| AGE GROUP | NUMBER OF TEACHERS AND ADULTS |
| --- | --- |
| Infant Care | One fully qualified teacher for every twelve infants with one adult for every four infants |
| Toddler | One fully qualified teacher for every twelve toddlers with one adult for every six toddlers |
| Preschool | One fully qualified teacher for every twelve preschoolers (twenty-four months to kindergarten) with one teacher and one aide for every fifteen preschoolers |
| School Age | One fully qualified teacher for every twenty-eight children with one adult for every fourteen children |

Source: State of California

## The Hours

Child care centers are typically open year-round with long hours so that parents can drop off and pick up their children before and after work. Most centers have both full-time and part-time staff who work staggered shifts in order to cover the entire day. Full-time employment is defined as thirty-five hours per week, fifty weeks per year. Often only one teacher remains in a classroom during the first and last hour of the day when few children are at the center.

## The Duties

Most teachers in child care centers spend their days teaching and providing basic care. Teachers of infants and toddlers not only change diapers and feed children, they also provide a variety of experiences to enrich the children's development. As children grow older, teachers are able to concentrate more on their social, emotional, physical, and mental development and less on basic care. They plan activities so that there is a balance between quiet and active periods and individual and group activities. Teachers at extended day-care programs work with school-age children supervising their care and homework and providing recreational activities.

# A Look at Different Child Care Centers

One of the best ways to understand the diversity of child care centers is to discover what several centers are like. Here are brief descriptions of four different child care center operations.

## Hacienda Child Development Center

The difficulty for working parents in finding quality care for their children can result in absenteeism from work, tardiness, lessened productivity in the workplace, and high employee turnover rates. Many employers have become aware of the issues involved in finding good child care, and some have taken steps to help their working parents. Some companies have established day-care centers on-site or nearby. Other companies offer benefits that pay for part or all of their employees' child care fees. And some companies offer referral services to help employees find quality child care programs.

The Hacienda Child Development Center, which is located in the Hacienda Business Park in Pleasanton, California, is an example of an outstanding child care facility situated just minutes from participating workplaces. The center was built by the Prudential Property Company as an amenity for its Hacienda Business Park at a cost of $3.2 million. Employees working in the Hacienda Business Park receive a discount on fees, as do employers who become corporate associates.

The seventeen-thousand-square-foot Hacienda Child Development Center has received international recognition for its innovative design. The center has eight classrooms for its program, which caters to children from infancy through elementary school. There are forty-five full-time teachers and regular substitute teachers. The classroom staff is composed of head teachers, lead teachers, and teachers. All receive a salary based upon education and experience. The center offers a benefits package that includes medical, dental, and 401(k) plans.

The Hacienda Child Development Center is open five days a week from 7 A.M. to 6 P.M. and operates year-round on a business calendar. The majority of children attend the center full-time. The center is operated by Early Learning Institute (ELI), which is a leader in providing quality child care services to working families, employers, and developers through its HeadsUp Child Development Centers Division. ELI, which was incorporated in 1982, operates its own centers as well as private centers under management contracts.

## Step One School

The Step One School is a nonprofit, public-benefit corporation governed by a board of directors. Step One has an open admissions policy, accepting applications on a first-come, first-served basis with adjustments for age and sex. The center is located in Berkeley, California, on a magnificent site overlooking San Francisco Bay. The building houses five sunny and airy classrooms, a kitchen, and a spacious, fenced play yard with areas for climbing, sand play, bike riding, and sitting on a deck under a tree. The shrub-covered hill has trails for hiking and exploration as well as an area for gardening.

The center offers these three programs:

- **Two-Year-Old Program** for ages two through two years and nine months, with a one-to-six teacher-child ratio

- **Nursery School Program** with mixed-age grouping for children two years and ten months through four years and eight months old, with a one-to-seven teacher-child ratio
- **Kindergarten Program**, a very individualized program with flexible groupings and a teacher-child ratio of one to twelve

The center maintains the same schedule for the children each day but remains sufficiently flexible to meet the children's changing needs. Each day the children's time is divided between (1) free choice of activities, both inside and outside; (2) small group activities such as stories, music, movement, drama, or walks; and (3) a daily group time for music, which includes all the children in a given classroom. Children have opportunities for a range of social experiences during the day by playing in unstructured groups, structured groups (large and small), and alone. The curriculum is planned week by week at classroom team meetings in which the events and progress of the last week are evaluated and new projects are developed collectively.

At present, approximately 125 children participate in the Step One program. About 50 percent come only in the morning, while 30 percent stay until 3 P.M. and 20 percent stay the entire day. The center is led by codirectors, and there are twenty teachers, of whom 50 percent work a part-time schedule of five to six hours per day. The teachers receive a monthly salary that includes overtime for meetings and conferences. The center offers a flexible benefits plan that teachers can apply to health, dental, dependent day care, retirement, and miscellaneous benefits. No benefits are offered to families, but this plan lets the employees put their benefits where they want them.

## Kid Time

Kid Time is a small, for-profit child care center that was established in the mid-1980s by one of the three stockholders, Steve

Wilson. He had been running a YMCA program for children and truly enjoyed it, so he decided to found his own school to provide quality child care. The center is open five days a week from 6:30 A.M. to 6:30 P.M. It is licensed for forty children who are cared for by three full-time teachers, two part-time teachers, and two part-time aides. The teachers are paid an hourly salary and receive medical benefits even though the center is small. The center provides five sick or personal days, two weeks of vacation after one year of employment, and paid holidays.

The center prides itself on offering quality child care in a homey center. Kid Time is located in an old home in a residential neighborhood. The house has been renovated, with an addition put on to make it appropriate for child care. There is a large room for classes; a room for the two-year-olds; plus a kitchen, bathroom, and utility and art room.

The center has classes for two-year-olds and young three-year-olds, three-year-olds and four-year-olds, and prekindergarten four-year-olds and five-year-olds. The morning program is preschool in nature, while the afternoon program includes naps for those who want them, some preschool activities, and free play. The center is devoted to developing the children's interactive language skills and social skills so they can function effectively with adults and peers.

## AmeriCorps and Child Care

A new opportunity for working in child care has emerged with AmeriCorps, the new national service program. Throughout the country, AmeriCorps members are either working directly with children in child care centers or training and recruiting new child care providers.

In exchange for their services, AmeriCorps members receive a stipend along with many educational opportunities. To learn more about all the opportunities that AmeriCorps offers and to get applications to join AmeriCorps, see the Appendix.

# A Look at Staff in Child Care Centers

Your duties as a teaching assistant, teacher, assistant director, or director will be similar at all child care centers—but not exactly the same. The following profiles provide a good picture of what it is like to work at these jobs in several child care centers. Where an individual starts on the career ladder at a center generally depends on his or her level of experience and education. The entry-level position is as an assistant teacher or aide, which usually leads quickly to a position as teacher after gaining sufficient experience and/or completing the proper course work.

Larger centers with several teachers in a classroom often designate a lead teacher. Besides teaching, this teacher coordinates the efforts of all the teachers in the room. At times the head teacher takes care of most of the administrative functions as well as consults with parents. Lead teachers are also called head teachers. At many child care centers, especially smaller ones, the director often teaches part of the time in addition to handling administrative chores. Directors are almost always chosen from the ranks of experienced teachers. Assistant directors are typically found at large centers and may or may not have teaching responsibilities.

## What It's Like to Be an Assistant Teacher at a National Chain

Jane Kocourek is on the bottom rung of the child care center staff ladder. She is an assistant teacher at a center that is part of a national chain. Her pay is hourly, and her benefits include health and dental insurance and optional life insurance and 401(k) plans. Jane holds a teaching certificate for kindergarten through sixth grade and taught kindergarten for three years in Minnesota. Because she did not have the early childhood education courses needed in California to be a teacher, she had to start as an assistant.

The general guidelines for Jane's workday are spelled out by the national chain. She works from 8 A.M. to 5 P.M. with a teacher in a self-contained room caring for eight one-year-olds. The room has

seven cribs, sleeping pads, a good supply of blocks, dress-up out-
fits, a play kitchen, manipulatives, and a wide variety of toys.

At the start of the day, Jane is usually sitting on the floor with
one or two of the young children playing, talking, or reading to
them. At around 9 A.M., Jane gives the children a snack, then they
go outside in the playground to play until lunch is served at 10:30
A.M. A cook prepares the lunch, and, as Jane or her partner teacher
serves the lunch, the other caregiver sits with the children and provides feeding assistance, if necessary. After lunch, the children
have a short stint outdoors before they are diapered and put down
for their naps. During nap time, Jane and the other caregivers take
the dishes back to the kitchen, collect the garbage, and wash each
child's cup or bottle. Also, Jane sets up sleeping cots for the older
children.

After her lunch, she checks with the assistant director and director to find out what else needs to be done that day. Sometimes she
supervises a group of sleeping children. At other times, she might
trace letters for a bulletin board. When the children start to wake
up at around 2 P.M., she returns to her young charges and reads or
plays quietly with them until all are awake. She may have them
play with clay or do movements to music. Then it is time for
everyone to be diapered again before a snack is served. After snack
time, the children play outside. When they return to the classroom, Jane coordinates individual activities with them until their
parents arrive.

Although Jane's workday is supposed to end at 5 P.M., she cannot leave until the number of children is four or fewer. She is paid
overtime for working after 5 P.M. During the day, Jane and the
other teacher informally share tasks.

Jane always wanted to be a child caregiver. As a five-year-old,
she would gather all the neighborhood toddlers to play in her
yard. Throughout her life, whenever she served as a volunteer or
had a job, it was always associated with children. She's been a day-
care volunteer, a camp counselor, and a children's church program
director. When Jane obtains her California teaching license, she

plans to leave the child care center to teach kindergarten. Jane would like to work with older children in the job she has studied to do, and the low wages at the child care center do not adequately support her.

## What It's Like to Teach at a Large Child Care Center

Alice Bush is a teacher at the Hacienda Child Development Center, a large, for-profit child care center that was specifically designed for the parents who work in the business park. Her classroom has thirty children between the ages of three and six. Besides Alice, there is a head teacher, a lead teacher, and another teacher. At all times, the ratio of children to teachers must be twelve to one to meet state requirements. However, the school tries to keep the ratio at ten to one. Besides teaching part of the time, the head teacher handles administrative duties and parent conferences and develops some of the classroom's curriculum. The lead teacher's job is to oversee everything in the classroom, to coordinate the afternoon program, and to teach full-time.

Alice's teaching day begins at 11 A.M. and ends at 6 P.M. Occasionally, she comes in earlier to substitute in the morning, if necessary. When Alice arrives, all of the children are outside. She spends her time making sure they are safe and may set up a game or do a special project with them, but, basically, she is just supervising a free-play period. At 11:30 A.M. the children return to the classroom, where one teacher reads to the children as the others direct bathroom time and set the room up for lunch and nap time.

After supervising lunch, which the children bring and eat in the room, Alice stays in the room with the nappers while the older children leave to participate in a kindergarten program. This is not idle time, as she is busy preparing the daily reports for the parents, developing materials, and making snacks. At 3 P.M., Alice and the nappers go back outside, where the children join again with the kindergarten group and have a snack. For an hour, the children enjoy free-choice activities, although Alice may at times lead them in a low-key game. All the children return to the classroom at 4 P.M. Many parents start to pick up their children at this time, so one of the teachers leaves. Between 4:30 P.M. and 5 P.M., the children do art, movement, or music under Alice's direction. At 5 P.M. and 5:30 P.M., the other teachers leave, depending on how many children are still in the classroom. Alice then supervises the children as they play with manipulatives, Legos, and blocks and talks to parents who have come to get their children.

Alice became hooked on working in child care and the Montessori method of teaching young children while working at a center with a Montessori program the summer she graduated from high school. Her interest in young children continued through college, where she obtained a B.S. in child development and worked part-time at a Montessori school. While she was in college, she also took thirteen units of Montessori training from a college extension program. She then worked part-time for six years at a Montessori school. The pay was poor and she had no benefits, but Alice was so dedicated to children that she worked weekends and even acted as janitor when necessary. A change in management plus the need to make more money resulted in a short stint as a secretary. Then Alice saw an ad in the newspaper for her present position, and she was hired.

What Alice likes about working at the Hacienda Child Development Center is the businesslike attitude of the administrators. She has a formal contract, is paid well for her work, and has good benefits. She does, however, find herself doing more paperwork than at her previous job. Her current plans include staying in the child care field as a teacher because she is absolutely committed to helping young children learn.

## What It's Like to Be an Assistant Director at a National Chain

Suzanne Cox works as the assistant director of one of the centers of a very large national chain of child care centers. Her day begins at 8 A.M., lasts until 5 P.M., and is filled with great diversity. As an assistant director, Suzanne must be able to step in and handle any task, including acting as director. Her routine duties include:

- posting all tuition payments
- handling the banking
- keeping the school's books
- organizing all the children's files
- keeping track of immunization records
- administering prescribed medicine to children
- preparing accident reports
- documenting and conducting fire drills
- contacting parents of sick children
- driving a van
- stepping in as a substitute teacher

Besides her regular duties, Suzanne takes on projects. For example, she has written a new program for the many prekindergarten children at the center who are natives of other countries. And in the course of stepping in where she is needed, she has frequently been a substitute teacher and was even the cook for a while until a new one was hired.

When Suzanne reentered the workforce, she chose child care because she did not wish to be separated from her youngest child. She took early childhood education courses and was soon working at the center where she is now assistant director. Suzanne had seen the center being built and just walked in and asked for a job. She had to start as a part-time, hourly aide because she had no experience in child care except raising her own children and had completed only three units of early childhood education courses. Her daughter also started at the center at the same time. Within just a few months, Suzanne became a full-time teacher after completing nine units of early childhood education courses at night. Within six months of starting at the center, Suzanne's expertise was recognized, and she became the assistant director.

Working at a national chain means receiving benefits, which is important to a working mother, plus earning what is considered a good salary for the child care field. Suzanne especially appreciates being able to have her daughter with her at her workplace. She also truly enjoys working with her director because they act as a team and anticipate each other's needs.

## What It's Like to Direct an Independent Child Care Center

Adrienne Lough is the director of Kid Time, a small, independent child care center. She arrives at the center at 6:15 A.M. and is the main caregiver until 8:30 A.M. for children arriving early. When her caregiving stint is over, she concentrates on administrative tasks. Although her workday is officially over at 2:30 P.M., she typically finds herself on the job until 3 P.M. or even 4 P.M. As director, it is her responsibility to see that the children receive quality care and that the teachers are responsible, loving caretakers. Her job includes overseeing teachers and their projects, filling in as a substitute teacher, hiring and firing teachers, handling enrollment of new children, advertising the center, shopping and ordering materials, attending monthly staff meetings and parent-teacher conferences, and relating to all parents on a one-on-one basis. Her day is so busy that she often eats lunch with the children.

Adrienne's entire career has been spent working with young children at child care centers. Her first job was part-time at a church-operated center while in college studying for her associate's degree in child development. After marriage, she worked at another center for two years, advancing to head teacher. She applied for her present job when she was living down the street from the center. The owner was so impressed with her qualifications that she hired Adrienne as assistant director and teacher. Adrienne learned how to be an assistant director from on-the-job training by the owner, who also served as the director, and from administrative courses she was required to take.

After working as the assistant director for one year, she took over the director's role. Adrienne has an abiding love for preschool children and thinks her job as the director of the center is great because she is able to work with children in a comfortable, homey atmosphere. In the future, she plans to finish her degree in child development, and someday down the road she may open her own child care center.

## Earnings

Child care center workers are definitely not well-paid. Of course, there are centers that do pay a satisfactory wage; nevertheless, most workers receive very low wages. The median hourly earnings of child care workers are less than $8.00 per hour. The lowest 10 percent earn less than $6.00 per hour, and the highest 10 percent earn close to $11.50 per hour. Figure 2 shows how the earnings of child care workers compare to those in other occupations.

Besides receiving low wages, child care workers receive minimal benefits. Some centers offer a full benefits package, including health insurance and paid vacations, but most offer no benefits at all. Many centers do offer free or discounted child care to employees. In addition, some offer seminars and workshops to help workers learn new skills.

## Employment Outlook

Opportunities for employment in child care centers are excellent. This is one of the fastest-growing occupations in the country. While an unusually large number of these jobs will come from the need to replace experienced workers who leave this career, demand for child care services is also increasing as more and more women continue to enter the workforce. Plus, the government is increasing subsidies to enable children from low-income families to attend day-care programs, so more children will participate in

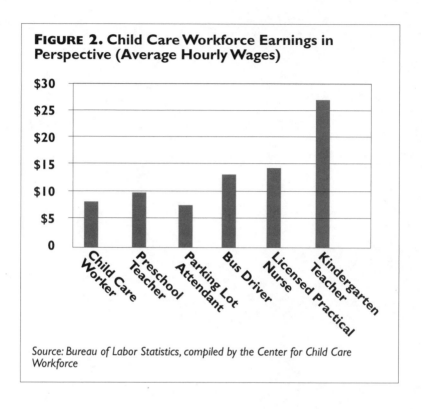

**FIGURE 2.** Child Care Workforce Earnings in Perspective (Average Hourly Wages)

Source: Bureau of Labor Statistics, compiled by the Center for Child Care Workforce

these programs. In addition, more and more employers are funding and operating child care centers.

# The Importance of a Child Care Career

Quality child care is absolutely essential to working mothers. Without such care, they cannot easily stay in the workforce. Furthermore, in a country that considers children a valuable resource, the children deserve early childhood experiences that will help them develop to their fullest potential. Being on the staff of a child care center may not earn you great tangible rewards, but the intangible ones are immense for kids at heart and others who adore children.

# CHAPTER THREE

# At-Home Child Care Careers

*Definition: At-home child care is offered in the
private residence of the child care provider.*

More and more Americans are now choosing careers that let them work in their own homes. For those who adore children, a home-based child care business seems a perfect choice. More than one million people have chosen this career—most are women. If you choose this career, you will find the demand for your services is very high. The steadily increasing number of working mothers means that more and more home-based child caregivers will be needed each year. Demand is high because many families prefer to have their young children cared for in a home environment with just a few children rather than in child care centers that may care for more than one hundred young children. Besides, parents like the idea of their children having just one caregiver with whom they can emotionally bond. Parents are also seeking before- and after-school care for their school-age children, which adds to the demand for home-based care.

## Is Home-Based Child Care the Right Career for You?

You can roll out of bed in the morning and be ready for work in just a few minutes. You can have a career working all day with children—a dream come true for those who adore children. There are many advantages to having a career in home-based child care. At the same time, there are disadvantages. You need to examine both sides closely to determine if this is the career for you. Here are some of the advantages to operating a child care facility in your own home.

1. You have the opportunity to create the care program that you think is best for children.
2. You can set the hours that you work as well as choose your own vacation time.
3. If you have young children, you are able to be at home with them to guide them through childhood.
4. You can choose the number of children for whom you will care.
5. You can choose the age group of the children for whom you will care.
6. You do not have to commute to your job.
7. You are the boss of your own business.
8. You can to hire helpers who share your child-rearing philosophy.
9. You can determine the fees you will charge.
10. You can set your daily schedule.

As with all career choices, a career caring for children in your own home has some downsides. Let's look now at some of the disadvantages.

1. You may not earn as much money as you would like because the going rate for child care is low in your community.
2. Your clients may not always pay on time.
3. You may find it difficult to hire helpers for the hours you need them.

4. You may miss having significant contact with adults during the workday.
5. If your own children are at home with you, they may resent sharing their home and parent with other children.
6. You may find it necessary to work long hours to accommodate the needs of your clients.
7. You may have clients who do not pick their children up on time.
8. You will probably have to purchase your own health insurance and other benefits.
9. You have to devote space in your home to operating your business.
10. You need to spend time keeping accurate business records.

As you probably noted, some advantages are also disadvantages. For example, you are your own boss, but that also means having all of the responsibilities of running a business, such as buying liability insurance and keeping records for taxes. You may have the advantage of being able to set your own fee schedule, but the disadvantage is that it may not be realistic for your clients. When you are weighing these advantages and disadvantages, think also of others that you could list for yourself. Everyone's list will be slightly different.

## Who Will Help You Establish Your Child Care Business?

When you think of getting a license, setting up one or more rooms in your home for child care, and finding clients, the task of establishing your own home-based child care program may seem formidable. Fortunately, Child Care Resource & Referral (CCR&R) agencies in most communities throughout the country can provide valuable assistance. You can contact the National Association of Child Care Resource & Referral Agencies to find the agency located in your community:

National Association of Child Care Resource & Referral
Agencies (NACCRRA)
3101 Wilson Boulevard, Suite 350
Arlington, VA 22201
www.naccrra.net

These agencies emerged in the early 1980s to help parents find quality child care in their communities. Besides performing this vital service, they also assist child caregivers in setting up and improving their own programs. CCR&R agencies are nonprofit and are supported by local, state, and federal programs; private companies; charitable organizations; United Way agencies; service organizations and groups like the American Association of University Women; and individual donors. Although the range of services varies, what follows are some of the major services home-based child caregivers are offered.

- **Licensing Help.** Agencies hold orientation meetings to acquaint prospective home-based caregivers with the steps involved in obtaining a license. They also provide help in filling out the necessary forms, which can be a complicated process in some states.
- **Business Advice.** Agencies offer prospective caregivers start-up advice. For established caregivers, they hold meetings and classes that deal with such subjects as marketing, insurance, taxes, and record keeping.
- **Referral Service.** Agencies keep files on hundreds of licensed child care providers that detail where their homes are located and what type of services are offered. A registry of home-based providers that are exempt from licensing but have met certain standards may also be kept. Agencies use this information to refer parents to child care providers.

- **Provider Development.** Agencies help child care providers improve their services through orientation sessions, workshops, conferences, phone counseling, hotlines, newsletters, and technical assistance. Agency resource centers may also have toys, books, and equipment available to loan to providers.

## What It's Like to Work at a CCR&R Agency

Careers for kids at heart and others who adore children need not always be directly involved with children. Working at a CCR&R agency allows you to help parents select appropriate care for their children as well as offer caregivers help in providing the quality care parents want.

Phyllis Graser was the special projects coordinator of one of the offices of a Child Care Resource & Referral agency. The council is a private, not-for-profit corporation governed by a volunteer board of directors that represents the diversity of the community. The council's goal is to improve the availability, affordability, and quality of child care services through the creation of a comprehensive, integrated child care delivery system that allows for parental choice and is supported by a combination of public and private resources.

Phyllis worked at the referral agency from 9 A.M. to 3 P.M. five days a week. To accomplish the goal of her agency, she made referrals to parents and tried to update the list of providers every month. She also called parents who used the agency's resources to check if they had found caregivers or needed more help. For working parents, she held noon seminars on such topics of interest as discipline, nutrition, and separation anxiety. And once a month she conducted meetings for prospective family child care providers on the business aspects of starting up a child care service in their own homes. Caregivers also called to ask her about toilet training or what to do with a child who bites, so Phyllis broadened her background by taking child development courses and reading the stacks of materials that came across her desk on child care and children's issues. One-fourth of her time was spent working with a child care initiative project that was funded separately by five businesses. This involved trying to increase the number of care providers for infants and school-age children as well as contracting for CPR training and offering advanced training workshops for providers.

What Phyllis liked best about her job was being able to help working parents find quality care for their children and help caregivers to provide that care. While career advancement is possible to a position as an area manager for one of the offices or as deputy director or executive director of the council, Phyllis left this position to become an elementary school teacher.

# What's Involved in Setting up Home-Based Child Care

Before choosing to start caring for children in your home, you need to know exactly what is involved. Besides handling all of the business aspects, you need to develop a sound schedule of daily activities for the children as well as understand and follow all local rules and regulations. You also have to make your home safe for children and acquire all types of toys, games, and educational materials. Do remember that Child Care Resource & Referral agencies can provide sound advice on how to accomplish these tasks.

## Rules and Regulations

Each state has different rules and regulations governing home-based child care. You may live in a state with stringent requirements or one that has practically no requirements. For example, some states only require caregivers to register their homes as "family child care homes." Others require licensing that ensures that home child care providers meet certain standards in health, safety, and staffing. In either case, home safety inspections and criminal background checks are usually required of applicants. Let's look at what is required to get a home care license in the state of California, which has more demanding requirements than many states.

1. All adults over age eighteen in the home must be finger-printed and tested for tuberculosis.
2. Certain fire and safety standards for the house must be met.
3. For a small-home license, care is limited to eight children, provided two of the children are of school age or only four children are under age two.
4. For a large-home license, care is limited to fourteen children with no more than four under age two and an aide present for seven or more children.
5. All physical and humiliating punishment is prohibited.
6. Parents have the right to visit the home at any time.
7. Guns and ammunition must be safely locked up.
8. No smoking is allowed while children are on the premises.
9. Provider must have taken CPR and first aid classes.

In California, you do not need a license if you care for children from only one family. In this case, there are no fingerprint and TB clearances or adult-child ratio requirements. However, parents can require you to get a physical examination and TB clearance, present references, and offer a smoke-free environment.

Besides licensing and registration requirements, it is essential to find out what the local zoning requirements are in your area. Furthermore, in most communities, it is necessary to obtain a business license in order to operate a home-based child care facility.

## The Business Aspects of Child Care

When you care for children in your home, you have established a business. In order to operate your business successfully, you must set up business procedures and act like the professional you are. You also need to consider the following issues.

**Insurance.** You must make sure that your home insurance policy will cover the operation of a child care business in your home, as most will not. Obtaining liability insurance will protect you if you are sued because a child is injured in your home.

**Setting Fees.** You need to study your market carefully and set your fees appropriately. This means considering what other home-based child care providers in your area are charging, as well as considering the income level of the clients you will be serving. In a small community, you could earn as little as fifty dollars or less per child for a week's care, while in some city or suburban neighborhoods you might be able to earn more than $175 per child. Typically, fees are set highest for infant care, less for preschoolers, and even less for school-age children requiring fewer hours of care.

**Contracts.** By having parents sign a contract for your child care services, you can avoid many misunderstandings. A contract should spell out what rules parents must follow. Your fee structure should also be explained in the contract, including penalties for late payment, fees for extra services, and charges for late pickup of children.

**Marketing.** In order to get clients, you must market your services. You should always contact the local CCR&R agency so you can receive referrals. Newspaper ads can help you find clients, as can flyers placed on bulletin boards in churches, grocery stores, YMCAs, beauty salons, parks, and wherever parents of young children gather. Also, word of mouth can be an effective marketing tool, so caregivers should tell everyone from pediatricians to friends that they are starting an at-home child care business.

**Record Keeping.** Small businesses cannot keep records in a shoe box. They must be organized so that caregivers have records for doing their taxes and seeing how well their child care business is doing. The simplest way to keep track of financial records is to purchase an accounting ledger that allows you to record income and expenses. Of course, computer buffs can handle this task on their computers.

**Creating a Safe and Healthy Environment.** Homes must be made safe for children. Therefore, some things caregivers must do include locking up or storing all hazardous materials out of reach; covering electrical outlets with safety caps; putting knives, medicines, and matches out of reach or in locked cabinets; and locking up any guns or ammunition. Toys need to be well made, and toys with small parts that children can swallow should be avoided. All outside play structures and interior furnishings that the children will use must be sturdy. And, of course, caregivers should arrange all toys and materials so they are easily accessible to the children.

**Handling the Day's Activities.** The most important part of caring for children in your home is setting up a sound program that will interest them and at the same contribute to their social, emotional, physical, and mental development. Be sure to schedule time for indoor and outdoor play, as well as time for the children to play alone and with others. Definite times for resting, meals, and snacks should be set. And it is very important to take time each day to read and tell stories to the children and introduce them to art, music, dance, and movement activities. In order to develop the best possible program of activities, you need to learn about child development. You can do this by reading and taking classes. In addition, you can learn a lot about handling children by talking to other caregivers. Many areas have associations of home caregivers who meet monthly to discuss concerns.

## What It's Like to Be a Home-Based Care Provider

Maureen B. Chahin has just started her career as a home-based child care provider. She believes it is the perfect career choice, as it allows her to be with her young daughter full-time and also to use her years of experience as a preschool, kindergarten, and elementary schoolteacher. Maureen has the solid advantage of knowing how to work with young children. The start-up was easy because her home needed no alterations. The bottom level of her home was already ideal for child care, with a playroom, bathroom, separate room for the nappers, and a door to the play yard.

Her first step in launching her child care business, called Kid Kelly Play and Learn, was to attend an orientation class at the Child Care Resource & Referral agency in her community. She learned about the licensing process and was told that only five of the twenty-five prospective caregivers would complete the process. To meet the fire department's requirements for the license, she had to install more fire extinguishers, fire alarms, and smoke detectors. The entire license process was lengthy, but Maureen did receive a large-home license to care for twelve children.

While waiting to get her license, Maureen began to get ready for opening her home-based child care business. She attended a CCR&R class on business and purchased insurance. She bought a book from CCR&R that had packets of forms that she could use. From these forms she developed a parent contract. (See the sample CCR&R contract.) Her yard was landscaped to accommodate the children, and she bought sturdy toys and blocks. Then Maureen made up a handbook for parents that included a health history, medical documentation of injuries, emergency information, liability information, a parents' rights page, and a form permitting the administration of medication. Maureen hired her sister, who also had a baby, as her helper. She also considered getting a local high school student in the early childhood program to work part-time.

Once she had her license, Maureen began to market her business. She put her name and phone number in the homeowner's newsletter in her area, placed an ad in the local paper, talked to a friend who did child care, and distributed flyers at a nearby park and a few stores. Almost everyone who came to visit her home

## CHILD CARE CONTRACT

I agree to enroll my child _____ age
_____ in the _____ Family Child Care
Home, beginning on _____. I have received and
read the Family Child Care Home Rules and agree to com-
ply with all rules and responsibilities as stated. This contract
will be valid beginning _____. Two weeks'
notice by either party will be required in order to terminate
this contract. This contract will be revised on an annual basis.
Care will normally begin at _____ o'clock and end at _____
o'clock on the following days of the week: _____
_____.
Care will/will not include the following meals and snacks:
_____.
The charge for care of the child is $ _____ per _____.
Overtime charges are $ _____ per _____.
Parents are expected to pay full rates for holidays, absences,
and parent vacations. Additional charges will be accrued for
special dietary requests or damages to the contractor's
property. Payment to the Family Child Care Provider will be
made in advance. Parents are to provide the names of any
persons authorized to pick up children, medical and insurance information, and any special dietary or health concerns.
(Optional) Payment obligation is based on the hours parent
contracts to use child care.

Provider Signature_____Date _____

Parent Signature_____Date _____
Address/Phone

Parent Signature_____Date _____
Address/Phone

*Source: Contra Costa Child Care Council*

signed their children up for child care. Four children were signed up for full-day care and several for different part-time combinations. When Maureen knew the age level of the children she would be caring for, she created a daily schedule of activities for them.

Although Maureen has not been working long in the child care business, she feels confident that it was a good choice for someone who truly likes working with young children. The children for whom she is caring have already bonded with her, and she loves them. The only downside so far is having to change so many diapers because the children range in age from eighteen months to three and a half years.

## What It's Like to Operate a Home-Based Child Care Program

Many mothers start child care programs in their homes because they want to be with their young children. This is the reason Nicole (Niki) Brown, like Maureen, turned the lower level of her home into a child care business more than two years ago. To start Tender Hearts Day Care, she called the Division of Family Services in her state to get a packet that had the forms she would need to register her program with the state. In addition, the packet contained sample contracts and menus and information about food programs and regulations for home child care programs. Niki discovered that she had to complete a class in first aid and CPR and that each county has a Step Ahead Office that offers child care placement help. She put her name on the organization's mailing list so she could get newsletters telling of classes and training programs. A mentoring program also teamed new child care providers with veterans whom they could call for advice.

Niki is allowed twelve children in her program. The state allows caregivers to have only five or six children if they work alone; however, Niki has an assistant who comes in daily from 7:30 A.M. until 4:30 P.M. Niki's program has three children under sixteen months, and the other children range in age from eighteen months to four years. She has an infant room for the children younger than eighteen months and those who are not yet developmentally ready to be with the older children.

The day is very structured in Niki's program. The center opens at 7 A.M., with all children arriving by 8 A.M. to have breakfast. Breakfast varies from pancakes, waffles, cereal, French toast sticks, and Pop Tarts to scrambled eggs and sausage. After breakfast, the children clean up, use the bathroom, and enjoy free time until 9 A.M., when structured activities begin. Niki runs her program almost like a preschool. She makes daily curriculum plans for both the infants and the toddler classes. Her plans are so creative that the day goes by swiftly for the young children as well as for the caregivers. Let's look at the toddler activities for one day.

- 9:00 A.M.—Everyone sits down in a circle, sings a welcome song, and greets each other. Next, the children look at the calendar and tape a bunny on the current day. They sing the days of the week and talk about what month it is, then they sing the month's song. Next, they have a conversation about the weather using a weather chart.
- 9:30 A.M.—After a brief time to stretch to music, it is learning time. They talk about the subject of the month, such as birds, and work on letters, shapes, and numbers.
- 10:00 A.M.—The children begin work on the letter of the week and usually have a coloring page with this lesson. Learning centers are also set up around the room so the children can do puzzles, paint, use the chalkboard, and play with toys at this time.
- 10:45 A.M.—During free playtime, the children can watch a video related to the day's lesson or engage in their own activities.
- 11:30 A.M.—Children clean the area and wash up for lunch.
- 11:45 A.M.—Lunchtime.
- 12:00 P.M.—Niki either reads a story or plays music to calm the children down for nap time.
- 12:30 P.M.—Each child rests on his or her own mat.

- 3:30 P.M.—After bathroom time, the children enjoy a snack and engage in free play until they are picked up.
- 4:30 P.M.—The program ends.

When the children leave in the afternoon, they take all their papers with them. They also take a chart that Niki has done for each of them describing their activities for the day. (See sample chart.)

---

### TENDER HEARTS DAY CARE
#### What We Did Today

**What my diapers were:** *n/a*

| Time | Wet | BM |
| --- | --- | --- |

**How did I eat?**          **Bottles:** *n/a*

| Did not | Partial | Complete |
| --- | --- | --- |
|  | oatmeal |  |
|  |  | banana |
| ravioli |  |  |
|  |  | carrots |

**Other Activities:**

*We were busy today! The kids watched a Barney movie that Parker brought to start circle time. Thanks! We talked about what day it was, put up the 23rd raindrop, sang the days of the week and the months of the year. We talked about the weather today and reviewed the shapes and colors. We sang some songs and sang about bunnies. We had a lesson on big and little. Their activity papers were gluing the big egg with the big bunny and vice versa. They colored a watch for the letter this week, and for craft time they painted Easter eggs. They had puzzle and book time after lunch, and we read The Three Little Pigs. Wow! What a day!*

**Supplies Needed:**

---

## The Plusses and Minuses of This Career

One drawback to an at-home child care business is establishing the fine line between friendship and business with parents. Not all parents pay promptly or pick their children up on time. As a true kid at heart, Niki likes working with the children and appreciates the opportunity to watch them grow and build a good relationship with them. And when they say, "I love you, Niki," it makes it all worthwhile.

# Another At-Home Option—Being a Foster Parent

Another way to take care of children in your home is as a foster parent. The demand is overwhelming for individuals who will care full-time for children whose natural parents cannot provide adequate care. Foster parents care for one or more children under the supervision of a public or private social agency. They provide a family environment for the children in their care. Some children might stay in a foster home for a short time period and then rejoin their families or be placed in an adoptive home. A few children remain in foster homes until they are eighteen years old.

Foster parents must be licensed to care for children. They typically are reimbursed for the children's food and lodging, and there is a tax break when children remain in their homes for a full year and can thus be considered dependents. Medical care is provided. While being a foster parent can be a full-time job, it is not a way to support oneself, as the pay for the care is about equivalent to the cost of caring for the children.

## Requirements for Becoming Foster Parents

**Licensing.** You need a license to be a foster parent. You can be single or married, but you must have sufficient income to support your family without relying on foster-care payments. You must be fingerprinted and pass a criminal background check and a general character interview. The requirements for your home are largely the same as for home-based child care. How many children you will be licensed to care for depends on the number of beds and bedrooms and the ages of the children. The state sets a maximum number of children that may be in the home at any one time.

**Personal Requirements.** You must be an extremely competent parent. All of the children for whom you will care have been taken from their families because the families cannot provide adequate care. Many will have been in four or more foster homes before coming to your home. You need to have excellent parenting skills so that you can handle their behavior and emotional problems and make these children feel secure in your home.

## What It's Like Being Foster Parents

Steve Warga and his wife, Karen, are currently foster parents to four children. Karen cares for the children full-time while Steve works. They have been caring for children for slightly more than three years and have already had seven children in their home. Steve can be labeled as an altruist. In the past, he has worked with people from troubled teens to convicts, so becoming a foster parent was a natural extension of his desire to help others.

Foster children do not just arrive on your doorstep. A social worker describes the child, and you can decide to accept or reject the child. You do have the opportunity to meet the child before making your decision. Steve says that a child's arrival in your home can be heartbreaking. Usually, all possessions are crammed into paper bags. The social worker brings the child to your home and stays for part of the day to help the foster parents and child adjust to each other. Steve remembers the arrival of Aaron, their first foster child, as one of the most emotional days of his life. He was literally shell-shocked from worrying about how he and his wife would cope with this four-year-old who had already been in several homes. Their bonding with Aaron, however, was fantastic. Steve and Karen are now adopting Aaron and his sister.

When children are placed in foster care, the first concern is their safety. Then the social workers try to resolve the case by reunifying the children with their natural parents when the parents can safely take care of them. If this doesn't happen, the next goal is adoption. If adoption is not possible, then a decision is made on the permanent placement of the children.

Besides Aaron and his sister, Steve and Karen are now taking care of two young children. A reunification plan has been drawn up for the sixteen-month-old boy, who may be able to return to his natural parents. The other child, a little girl, was prematurely born to a mother who was a substance abuser. Today, at seven months, she is plump and healthy and scheduled to be returned to her family. One of the most unfortunate aspects of being a foster parent is the temporariness of it. You bond closely with a child who becomes part of your family, and then the child must leave.

Besides being a foster parent, Steve has served as president of the local association of foster parents. This organization forms a support network for foster parents. Through monthly meetings, they are able to share problems and successes and dispel the stress that builds up from handling troubled children in their homes. Four times a year, there are countywide meetings where foster parents socialize and enjoy informational programs. As president of the organization, Steve also served as an advocate to governmental groups striving to improve the handling and financing of the foster-home program.

# Working in Group Homes

Another possible job for individuals wanting to work with children is being a child care worker in a group home. This is a job that allows you to spend almost all of your time interacting with children, as you may live at the group home. Your workplace could be a private home, one of many cottages at a large center, or in a large facility. There are group homes for children of all ages, whether they are foster children, mentally impaired children, or children with severe disabilities. At many group homes, you act in the place of the children's parents. This involves doing typical parental tasks such as getting the children to make their beds and helping them with homework. At other group homes, your relationship with the children may be more formal, with supervisors overseeing your work. Almost every group home needs child care workers. Furthermore, the number of group homes is growing as more organizations and special-interest groups are establishing homes. Entry-level workers, however, may only earn the minimum wage and may or may not receive benefits.

## Employment Outlook

Today, nearly two-thirds of all children under the age of six are cared for by someone other than their parents. Approximately 14 percent of these children are cared for in family child care homes. The number of homes offering this type of care exceeds three hundred thousand. While most of these homes are found in larger cities, even the smallest communities have home-based child care facilities. As the population of working parents, especially mothers, continues to increase, so does the need for more family child care homes. You can easily determine the demand for this service in your community by contacting the local Child Care Resource & Referral organization.

## The True Value of Caring for Children in Your Own Home

When you care for the children of working parents, you are giving the parents the opportunity to work without worrying about the well-being of their children. At the same time, you are giving their children a loving home environment in which they can develop to their full potential. When you care for foster children or children in group homes, you are giving them the opportunity to experience warm, caring parents. Your care for infants and toddlers is especially important as these are the years children learn about themselves and the world through their interactions with caring adults. Caring for children in your home or a group home gives you the opportunity to work with the children you adore and make a substantial contribution to their lives.

# CHAPTER FOUR

# Nanny Careers

*Definition: A nanny takes care of one or more children in the children's home, tending to their early education, nutrition, health, and other needs.*

Mary Poppins is the "practically perfect" nanny who changed the lives of the Banks children in a series of books by P. L. Travers and was brought to the silver screen by Disney. Nannies today are definitely not like the prim and proper, starched Mary Poppins that Julie Andrews portrayed in the movie. Furthermore, they are as different as night and day from the original British nannies who were taught at the internationally known Norland Nursery Training College in England.

If you decide to become a nanny, you will not be required to wear a starched black uniform with a white apron topped with a little black hat and sensible sturdy shoes or to take charge of afternoon tea in the nursery.

For a quick look at what today's nannies are like, just watch them in action on popular nanny TV programs as they turn dysfunctional families into happy ones. Nannies are as up-to-date as the latest sports star's shoes and are in just as much demand. We don't know how long the demand for a particular athlete's shoes will last, but we do know that the demand for nannies will remain high as long as there are working parents who want their children cared for in their own homes.

# The Demand for Nannies

You can easily see how high the demand for nannies is by studying newspaper ads. The following ads were placed in metropolitan areas with a population of more than one million. Note the range of positions that are available to nannies.

NANNY/MOTHER'S HELPER. Wanted for four wonderful children, ages three months to ten years. Seeking career nanny who enjoys travel. Family offers top salary and benefits. Passport, driver's license, and flex time needed.

NANNY. Live-in, full-time. Light housekeeping. Infant experience. References. Denver suburb.

NANNY, for eleven-month-old, in our Eastside condo. Twenty to thirty hours per week, plus occasional evenings. Nonsmoking. References required.

NANNY. Live-out. Care for infant and seven-year-old in Minneapolis home three days per week. Experience and references required. Own car required.

NANNY/HOUSEKEEPER. Live in our Los Angeles home, great hours.

The job description for a nanny will vary for each household. In one situation you might only supervise the activities of the children. In another you may be required to do light housekeeping and even prepare the evening meal for the entire family.

The demand for nannies far exceeds the number of graduates in this field. It is an excellent career opportunity for a long-term career. Travel with families and the experience of different cultures are exciting. The nanny can make an excellent income with room, board, and living expenses paid. There are also opportunities for nannies who wish to have a live-out position and/or raise families of their own. Although some families are willing to employ nannies who lack proper training, the professional nanny with a certificate will have better income potential, increased professionalism, and greater likelihood of career success and satisfaction.

# What Is a Nanny?

Nannies are not simply babysitters; they are usually highly trained professionals who are an extension of the family in the parents' absence. Most nannies work for families on either a live-in or live-out basis and take on all the jobs involved in caring for the children of the household. Usually, the tasks are restricted to child care and related domestic tasks.

The International Nanny Association (INA) has adopted minimum standards for nannies that state a nanny must be at least eighteen years of age, have completed high school or the equivalent, be in good health with proof of up-to-date immunizations, and, where required, have proof of negative TB test and/or chest X-ray. The one qualification that all nannies must also have is a genuine respect for and devotion to children, which makes being a nanny a perfect job for those who adore children.

# Aptitudes Needed for Being a Nanny

Being a nanny is a true profession. The International Nanny Association suggests that prospective nannies ask themselves these questions before deciding on this profession:

1. Do I really enjoy working with children?
2. Do I have something to contribute to children's lives?
3. Do I know the basics of child care?
4. Do I understand that children have different needs at different ages?
5. Can I handle an emergency?
6. Am I flexible?
7. Do I communicate well with adults and children?
8. Do I have a sense of humor?
9. Am I organized?
10. Do I use good common sense?

# Preparing to Be a Nanny

Take the time to contact the International Nanny Association if being a nanny is your career goal. This organization is a private, nonprofit educational organization for nannies and those who educate, place, employ, and support professional in-home child care providers. The International Nanny Association can provide solid career information on being a nanny. Read the organization's publications, "So You Want to be a Nanny" and "Recommended Practices for Nannies" to gain valuable insight into this profession. The organization also offers networking and professional growth opportunities, access to educational resources, a quarterly newsletter, an annual conference, and a wealth of additional materials. For more information, contact:

International Nanny Association
2020 Southwest Freeway, Suite 208
Houston, TX 77098
www.nanny.org

In order to be a good nanny, you need preparation. You can start by gaining actual child care experience by babysitting or working in a child care center. An increasing number of nannies obtain formal training and education to learn child care skills. Some earn bachelor's or associate's degrees in early childhood education. And many attend nanny training programs in private schools, vocational schools, and community colleges. Most community colleges now offer degrees in child development. Some high schools also offer courses in the child care field.

Typical training programs offer courses related to child care, including child growth and development, psychology, food and nutrition, health and safety, play activities, first aid, CPR, and family dynamics. Programs usually involve hands-on child care, and many provide basic information on personal health and grooming, etiquette, social skills, and professional development.

# Choosing a Nanny School

Nanny training schools are relatively new in the United States. Most were started in the 1980s to meet the overwhelming demand for trained nannies that emerged at that time. The International Nanny Association publishes the *Annual Directory of Nanny Training Programs*, which provides listings of schools and employment agencies. You can also contact local vocational schools and community colleges to find out if they have nanny training programs. Colleges that offer bachelor's degrees may not have courses that meet the special needs of nannies.

Before enrolling in a nanny school, you should carefully check out the merits of the school's program, according to Joy Shelton, former chairperson of the American Council of Nanny Schools. She offers the following suggestions to prospective students in assessing a nanny school:

1. Talk to graduates of the school about their experiences.
2. Talk to families that have hired students from the school.
3. Check with the Better Business Bureau and local chamber of commerce to make sure that there is no record of complaints against the school.
4. Check with the state department of education to see if the school is licensed by the state.

Furthermore, the International Nanny Association suggests asking these specific questions about the training program before you make your decision:

1. What specific courses does the curriculum include?
2. If the program requires work with children as part of the training, is the work supervised by an instructor?
3. What are the qualifications of the instructors?
4. How many students have completed the training program? Were they able to find jobs?

5. What is the capacity of the program? Average enrollment? Class size?
6. Is it possible to visit the school or sit in on a class?
7. What is the tuition refund policy if the student drops out of the course?
8. What is the percentage of students who complete the program versus the number who sign up for it?

# A Look at a Nanny School

The nanny certificate program at Vincennes University in Vincennes, Indiana, was established in 1992 to train professional nannies. The program is organized to stress maximum proficiency in specific child care skills and employment relations. The school provides a unique program divided equally between hands-on experience and academic training. The academic curriculum includes classes in areas such as child care and development, psychology, family relations, nutrition, childhood health and safety, and home management and family communications. Supervised field placements are provided at local day-care centers and private homes with children.

At Vincennes University, new classes start every year, and it takes one full academic year to complete the program. To be admitted to the school, a high school diploma or GED is required. The school is looking for individuals with no criminal record, an above-average driving record, no name on any child abuse rosters, no medical disabilities that would prevent them from lifting the children, and a clean drug and alcohol record. On the personality side, they want prospective students to demonstrate creativity, time management skills, initiative, responsibility, self-confidence, and a love of teaching and children. Here is a recent announcement describing the nanny program.

Graduates of the school are placed in homes across the United States. Openings are currently available in nearly all major cities and even many rural areas.

**FAMILY AND CONSUMER SCIENCES
PROFESSIONAL NANNY CERTIFICATE**
**A ONE-YEAR CERTIFICATE OF GRADUATION PROGRAM**

Intensive training program for child care professionals who will enter family homes and share in the responsibility of rearing their children. This program prepares students to meet the varied needs of the families they serve and integrate their lives with those of their employers. These duties could include adapting menus to special dietary needs, managing the day-to-day affairs of the household, aiding a handicapped or gifted child, and communicating with schools, parents, and children.

Students who wish to continue their education find that the Child Care Professional Nanny Certificate is the first step in their career ladder. The credits received at Vincennes University can be applied toward an associate's degree. This training can often be applied toward a degree in teaching or other child care professions.

Upon successful completion of thirty-one semester hours of specified courses, students receive a certificate of accreditation as a Child Care Professional Nanny from Vincennes University.

*NOTE: All students must satisfy the university's minimal requirements through either placement tests or enrollment in MATH 101, 103, 105, or 109. It is highly recommended that students achieve Red Cross life-saving certification or intermediate swimming proficiency.*

# Certification

Passing the Nanny Credential Exam given by the International Nanny Association is a way for nannies to demonstrate that they are top-quality professionals. It is recommended that nannies have two thousand hours of professional child care experience and current certification in infant/child CPR and first aid before taking the test. The test covers a nanny's knowledge in such areas as child development, child guidance, safety, learning environment, nutrition, and other related topics. For more information about the test, contact the International Nanny Association.

## Earnings and Benefits

A survey by the International Nanny Association in 2004 showed that live-in nannies earned an average of $532 per week and live-out nannies earned an average of $590. Nevertheless, earnings for some nannies can be considerably less or more. An experienced nanny may earn up to $1,200 a week, while an entry-level caregiver earns less than $500. A nanny's salary varies depending on many factors, including experience, job location, responsibilities, and training. In addition to a salary, many nannies receive paid health insurance, room and board, a car to drive, travel to exotic vacation spots, membership in health clubs, and an opportunity to attend college part-time. Some families even pay college tuition for their nannies, and many nannies have earned college degrees.

## What It's Like to Be a Nanny

Linette Caldwell, who became a nanny after graduating from college with a degree in social work, finds that she enjoys the feeling of being really needed but dislikes the long hours. See whether you would enjoy one of Linette's days.

- 7:00 A.M.—Ready for the day.
- 7:05 A.M.—See that the two oldest girls get on the school bus—they have already eaten their own cereal.
- 7:30–9:00 A.M.—Feed three children ages six, five, and three. Children watch television. Help kindergarten child with his speech. Children play as I clean house. Children help make beds then brush their teeth and get ready for preschool.

- 11:00 A.M.—Feed the three children lunch and take two of the children to preschool. Spend time with the remaining child. The children take turns going to preschool so that a different child gets individual adult attention from me each day. During this special time, the two of us might go to the park, read, or just play together.
- 3:30 P.M.—Everyone is home. Children do their chores, practice their music, and start their homework.
- 4:30 P.M.—The children play during the next two hours as I fix dinner and keep an eye on the three little ones.
- 6:30 P.M.—Family meal.
- 7:00 P.M.—Day is finished.

Linette points out that since she lives with the family five nights a week, sometimes it can be difficult to get away. Even though she has her own quarters on a lower floor, the two older children often find her and want to talk or need help with their homework. During the week Linette is not only responsible for the children, she also does the children's laundry as well as basic daily house chores. A housekeeper comes in once a week to wash the lunch and breakfast dishes and to make all three meals on that day.

Do you think that you could handle one of Linette's days? Linette found her job through a professional nanny agency.

## What It's Like to Run a Nanny Employment Agency

Genie Miller has always worked with children and has a degree in early childhood education with a minor in child psychology. She has been a teacher and director at a preschool, a library assistant, and a children's summer science camp director. Genie was also a frustrated working mother who could not find the quality care she wanted for her children without having to uproot them daily from their home environment and place them in a child care center. This gave Genie the idea to start her own nanny employment agency.

Indy Nannies Plus, the agency that she co-owns with Beth Gilman, was started in 1990. Since then, the company has had thousands of calls from clients interested in hiring nannies, demonstrating the tremendous demand. The agency acts as an intermediary by screening both the clients and the nannies. At no cost to the nanny, the nanny is given a physical, a TB test, and drug tests; is fingerprinted; has a criminal background and driving record check; and is trained in CPR.

Indy Nannies Plus requires individuals who wish to be placed as nannies to have two years of child care experience or a two-year associate's degree in order to be eligible for an agency interview. If you satisfy this qualification, you will be asked to fill out the application. Linette Caldwell met these qualifications and completed the necessary application. She was also required to write a "Dear Parent" letter to introduce herself to parents who might want to interview her. On the facing page is the letter that helped Linette obtain her current position.

## Interviewing for a Nanny Position

Every nanny has to learn how to handle interviews with prospective employers. Indy Nannies Plus holds interviews in which clients interview nannies selected by the agency. Each interview takes around thirty minutes. Here is a list of the questions that Linette had to answer in her interview:

1. What is your best quality?
2. Are you flexible?
3. Are you punctual?
4. What is your approach to discipline?
5. How many children do you feel comfortable caring for at one time?

Dear Parents,

Hi, my name is Linette. I am a twenty-four-year-old single female possessing caring, honest, and reliable attributes. I am laid back and flexible and try to possess an open mind at all times. Some of my interests include working out, walking, reading, and participating in outdoor activities. I hope to obtain a live-in nanny position in which two or three toddlers are involved. I prefer ages one and above but would not turn down an opportunity involving an infant.

I recently received my B.S. in sociology with a minor in criminal justice. I graduated from Iowa State University, where I had the opportunity to enroll in child development classes. I learned a lot about toddlers and their stages of development. I truly enjoyed these classes, and I hope to pursue a career involving toddlers. My future plans include returning to college to obtain my master's degree in early childhood development or family and marriage counseling.

My work history has allowed me to gain valuable experience. I have learned how to work as a team member and to accept responsibility for my own actions. Employers and coworkers have often complimented me on my ability to be efficient, confident, and dependable. Although my job experiences do not directly involve children, I feel they will give you a good idea of the kind of employee I would be.

In terms of experience with children, I come from a family with five brothers and six sisters. I fall right in the middle. During grade school and high school, I also had various babysitting jobs. I would be more than happy to provide you with the names of those people who employed me.

I sincerely hope you will consider me for an interview with you and your family. I strongly believe I will be a positive role model for your children.

Thank you for your time and consideration.

6. What ages of children do you prefer?
7. Tell me about your experiences with children. What did you like most? Least?
8. How long a commitment can you make?
9. How assertive are you?
10. Are you willing to care for children according to my philosophies?
11. What are some of the activities you like to do with children?
12. If you took them on field trips, where would you like to go?
13. How do you react to criticism?
14. Tell me about your background.
15. Do you know how to childproof a home?
16. Do you know the Heimlich maneuver?
17. Do you feel comfortable driving with children in the car?
18. What hours can you work?
19. Can you work overtime? Weekends? Travel with our family on vacations?
20. What are your feelings about light housework?
21. What do you consider light housework to be?
22. Why do you want to be a nanny?
23. How many days did you miss from your job last year?

The agency always suggests that a second interview be held in the client's home so that the client will be able to see how the nanny interacts with the children. If a perfect match is made, both nanny and client return to the office to negotiate a contract. It is important that both parties understand the job. Everything must be spelled out clearly in the contract. Note the specific provisions in the contract on the facing page.

## Nanny Code of Conduct

The International Nanny Association has adopted a Code of Conduct to promote professionalism and ethical practices among nannies, educators, and those who employ and place in-home

## EMPLOYER/NANNY CONTRACT

This agreement is entered into between _____
(employer) and _____(nanny).
The employer seeks to secure the nanny as a professional
child caregiver, and nanny wishes to provide such services.
Employer's Address _____
Telephone_____ Zip Code _____
Employer's Child(ren):
Name _____ Age _____
Name _____ Age _____
Name _____ Age _____
Nanny's Address_____
City/State/Zip _____
Telephone _____
Nanny's Social Security Number _____

**Compensation:**
Salary _____Hourly Pay _____
Overtime _____ Holiday Pay _____
Scheduled Hours _____ Days _____
Nanny is to receive _____Vacation Days
Paid Vacation: Yes ___No ____    Paid Holidays: Yes ___No ___
Nanny is to receive the following holidays:_____

**Duties:**
Child Care _____
Household _____
Errands _____
Other _____

**Termination:**
Nanny agrees to pay employer $ _____ if the nanny quits
before _____. Nanny will give _____ weeks' notice prior to
leaving employment. Employer will give nanny _____ weeks'
notice and $ _____ severance pay to terminate agreement.

Nanny's Signature _____ Date _____
Employer's Signature _____ Date _____

child care specialists. By virtue of their membership in the International Nanny Association, members agree to abide by this Code of Conduct and to support quality in-home child care for the world's most valuable resources—our children.

## Responsibilities to the Child

A nanny shall:

- Respect each child as a human being and never knowingly participate in any practice that is disrespectful, dangerous, exploitive, intimidating, or psychologically or physically harmful.
- Maintain a safe and healthy atmosphere that encourages optimum social, emotional, intellectual, and physical development of children.
- Provide various learning opportunities through which a child can explore and utilize his or her continued personal growth and development.
- Recognize the unique potential of each child, encourage questions, and present answers that children can understand.
- Keep abreast of current activity in the areas of childhood development through continued education, either formally or informally.
- Work toward promoting knowledge and understanding of young children and their needs and act as an advocate for children's rights.
- Be familiar with the signs of child abuse and neglect and be knowledgeable of procedures for dealing with them.

## Responsibilities to the Parents

A nanny shall:

- Treat parents and other family members with respect by maintaining confidentiality and respecting the family's right to privacy.

- Work together with parents to create an environment conducive to the healthy development of the child.
- Respect the family's child-rearing values and parents' rights to make decisions for their children.
- Support the family's value system, cultural expression, and individual characteristics and refrain from imposing personal values or biases upon the child.
- Be an advocate for children and work to protect their rights.
- Not hold the child accountable for negative interactions between parents and nanny.
- Inform parents of physical injury, illness, and emotional crises should they occur in the child's life.

## Responsibilities to Self

A nanny shall:

- Present herself or himself as an acceptable adult role model, take pride in personal appearance and professional behavior, and refrain from any activity that might injure credibility or produce a negative representation of herself or himself or an employer.
- Continue to improve personal knowledge of child development by seeking contemporary information through formal or informal means, such as membership in child care organizations.

# The Au Pair Experience

Nannies are take-charge people who are completely responsible for the care of children. Au pairs also live with families and provide help with child care and light housework. They usually work under the direct supervision of the parent and may or may not have previous child care experience. Au pairs work from forty to sixty hours a week. Besides American au pairs, there are foreign au pairs who live in the United States for up to a year to experience American life. They live as part of the host family and receive a small allowance or salary and help with child care and housework. Americans can also work abroad, usually in Europe, as au pairs to experience the culture of another country.

## The Rewards of Being a Nanny

Remember how the Banks family loved Mary Poppins? The modern nanny receives the same outpouring of feelings from families. And if you adore children, being a nanny is an opportunity to spend all your working hours with children. Furthermore, it is an opportunity to help young children develop successfully in their own warm family environment.

# CHAPTER FIVE

# Babysitting Careers

*Definition: A babysitter cares for children in the children's home or in the sitter's home on a part-time or full-time basis but is not licensed or approved by local, county, state, or federal guidelines.*

The test of being a great babysitter is being asked back again and again because the children love you. A babysitter can be a teenager who simply adores children or an adult who is truly a kid at heart. It is a special job that lets you choose your hours and workdays as well as work for several different families. You'll even be able to dress casually for work. Plus, the job can be fun as it gives you the opportunity to play with children while you are watching them. Approximately one million people in the United States are currently working as babysitters.

## Training for Babysitters

The more skilled you are as a babysitter, the more clients you will have, and the more money you will earn. Well-qualified babysitters know the importance of learning all they can about taking care of children. They must be ready to perform the Heimlich maneuver on a choking child, handle a child with an upset stomach, or treat a sprained ankle. These skills do not come naturally; they are learned through classes through YMCAs, high schools, vocational schools, community colleges, and the Red Cross.

Child care classes give you practical training in health and safety and important information about child development. They provide instruction on how to prevent injuries and reduce the spread of infectious diseases. You learn how to recognize and care for common childhood illnesses. And you learn how to improve your skills in communicating with children and their parents.

The American Red Cross has produced, in cooperation with the American Academy of Pediatrics and with review from the National Academy of Sciences, the first and only national program designed for children's caregivers. The Child Care Course is taught by certified instructors who present the information in an easy-to-follow format through group discussions, videos, demonstrations, role playing, and short lectures. You take away from the course a handy, attractive workbook that is a ready resource whenever you are caring for young children.

The Child Care Course takes fifteen hours to complete. The first eight hours are devoted to pediatric CPR and first aid. Participants earning 80 percent or better on the written CPR test receive certification in CPR for one year. Those passing the first aid test with 80 percent or better earn first aid certification for two years. The remaining seven hours of the course are devoted to preventative health and safety. For satisfactorily completing this part of the course, participants receive a certificate.

The Red Cross also offers a babysitting course designed for eleven- to fifteen-year-olds that helps them:

- interview for a babysitting job
- choose safe and age-appropriate toys and games
- perform first aid
- learn diapering and feeding techniques
- handle bedtime issues
- learn tips for having a safe babysitting experience

## Special Qualifications Babysitters Need

Taking classes and learning how to care for children is no guarantee that a prospective babysitter will be an excellent sitter. Certain special qualifications are needed. You must be a kid at heart who has the patience to play endless games of Candyland and Chutes and Ladders with your young charges. Babysitters should also have the stamina to survive marathon sessions of ping-pong or Nintendo. Another requirement is to be a nurturing individual who feels genuine affection for children and truly enjoys cuddling fractious infants and young children. You need the confidence to handle children from infants to preteens. Finally, having a cool head in a crisis is an absolutely essential babysitting skill, as you must respond calmly in emergencies.

## Babysitters' Responsibilities

On the job, babysitters have several responsibilities from the moment they enter a home. Their major responsibility is to watch the children, which includes:

- playing with the children
- preventing accidents
- selecting safe and appropriate toys and games for each child
- giving the children your undivided attention
- changing diapers of infants and toddlers
- bathing and dressing infants and young children
- feeding babies
- fixing meals or snacks for the children
- cleaning up messes
- handling the household

If a babysitting job is going to be long-term, the babysitter must meet with families ahead of time to establish what their guidelines and expectations are.

On first-time assignments as well as subsequent jobs, babysitters need to secure the following vital information before the parents leave:

- general behavior guidelines
- rules on television viewing and snacking
- children's official bedtime
- special duties to be performed, such as bathing or feeding the children, doing dishes, and so forth
- telephone number or information on how to reach the parents in case of an emergency

For all jobs, babysitters need to know where the following items are located in the home:

| | |
|---|---|
| flashlight | paper towels |
| tissues | clock |
| candles | telephone |
| matches | cleaning supplies |
| first aid kit | pencils and pens |
| vacuum cleaner | writing paper |
| sponge | thermostats |

Some babysitters watch children in their own homes. They have the additional responsibility of making their homes child safe.

## The Business of Babysitting

Most babysitters find jobs through people they know and by advertising their services on bulletin boards and in newspapers. Some babysitters work for agencies that assign them to jobs. To avoid misunderstandings, babysitters need to discuss their standard fees as well as payment required for extra services beyond routine child care before they begin to sit. Earnings are based on community standards. A babysitter in New York City or Chicago will earn more than one in rural North Dakota.

Earnings are typically based on an hourly rate. However, older, more experienced babysitters are able to charge more for their services than their younger, less-experienced counterparts. For example, a teenager in a major metropolitan area might earn $10 an hour while an experienced adult would earn between $10 and $20 per hour. In addition, babysitters frequently receive tips for their services.

# What It's Like to Be a Babysitter

Amy Bauerle started babysitting in high school to earn money. The hours fit into her schedule because the children she watched were in school at the same time she was. Amy liked children and had a younger brother who called her his "second Mom," so Amy believed that babysitting would be appealing to her. She knew she was good at thinking of imaginative things to do with children and enjoyed playing with them. Several other factors sold her on babysitting: the setting was casual rather than a formal office, there was no dress code, and her only obligations were to keep the children safe and stay within their parents' behavior guidelines.

Amy currently babysits two school-age girls who are eight and six. She secured the job because she was a peer facilitator during her senior year in high school. This involved spending six weeks learning what to expect from children, plus developing good communication skills with children. Each peer facilitator was matched with five different children who shared common interests with the facilitator.

As a peer facilitator, Amy visited a different child every day at the child's school, becoming the child's friend and assisting the child with any problem, including homework. She was there to help each child express or learn how to express his or her emotions in a healthy and acceptable fashion.

Amy's only training for being a babysitter was caring for a younger brother and watching the things her mom did with him. However, she does feel that her child psychology, early child development, and peer facilitating classes increased her knowledge of how to deal with children in different situations and taught her what to expect from them.

On a typical day during the school year, Amy picks the girls up at their school and drives them home. After a snack and a chat about their day, she supervises their homework. On the days the girls have lessons, such as horseback riding and gymnastics, Amy drives them to their lessons. If one girl has a lesson at a different time, the other girl and Amy spend some special time together. Each evening, part of Amy's job as a babysitter is to start preparations for dinner. Amy's job ends when the girls' mother arrives home from work between 6 P.M. and 7 P.M. In the summer Amy spends a full day with the children, beginning at 7:30 A.M. and ending at about 6 P.M. She has the responsibility for all their meals and activities during the day. Quite often, she drives them to lessons or to a pool. Amy describes these days as a relaxed time for her and the children.

Amy advises babysitters on the importance of asking many questions on the first day of a new job to learn the children's routines and the parents' expectations. This is also the time when babysitters need to have a frank conversation with parents to establish pay and the rules the children are to follow. As a babysitter, Amy is paid an hourly wage plus bonuses for running errands. She especially likes the job because it fits in with her school schedule and because she is a kid at heart who truly enjoys being around children.

## What It's Like: Getting Started as a Babysitter

Kitty Quisser is only in junior high school, but she knows that she adores children and has dreamed for years of being a babysitter. She started babysitting for her mother, who then told other people about her, and they started hiring her as a babysitter. Kitty's preparation for becoming a babysitter included Red Cross courses in babysitting plus the sitting she did for her own family. On her very first job, Kitty knew at once that babysitting was the career for her, as she thoroughly enjoyed playing games, riding bicycles, and watching a movie with her charges. Kitty attributes her confident attitude toward her work to her solid preparation for babysitting.

## The Need for Babysitters

Babysitters give parents worry-free workdays because they know that their children are being carefully watched. They allow parents to have a few carefree hours of togetherness or a vacation without the company of their children. America's children need you, the trained babysitter, to help them grow and develop into healthy, happy people when their parents cannot be with them. Your job is important. After all, our children are our future.

# CHAPTER SIX

# Teaching Careers

*Definition: A teacher is one whose occupation is to help children learn and apply concepts.*

Preschool, kindergarten, and elementary school teachers play a vital role in the development of children. What children learn and experience during their early years can shape their views of themselves and the world and can affect their later success or failure in school, work, and their personal lives. It is these teachers who introduce children to mathematics, language, science, and social studies. They use textbooks, games, music, artwork, films, books, computers, and other tools to teach these basic skills. In today's increasingly technological world, what children need to know grows exponentially every year.

Just imagine what the world would be like if we didn't have the knowledge, skills, and ideals of the past that teachers bring to us. Few people in today's high-tech world could learn enough on their own to get along.

More people belong to the teaching profession than any other. It is a noble profession with a long list of stellar names, from Socrates and Aristotle, who instructed the ancient Greeks, to Jaime Escalante, who taught calculus to children who had never dreamed they were capable of mastering the complexities of advanced mathematics. If you are interested in providing the tools and environment for children that can affect how well they succeed in their lives, then teaching may be the career for you.

## Is Your Personality Right for Teaching?

Not everyone has the personality to be a teacher. In your own experience at school, you have probably had teachers who made learning come alive and made you eager to come to school each day. Take the following quiz to find out if you share the same traits most successful teachers have.

1. Do you enjoy being with children?
2. Are you patient with children?
3. Can you keep your cool when things go wrong?
4. Do you get satisfaction from helping others?
5. Do you have a pleasant-sounding voice?
6. Do you have a high energy level?
7. Are you able to adapt to a new situation quickly?
8. Are you able to control a group of children?
9. Are you an imaginative and creative person?
10. Do you enjoy planning activities for children?

The more questions you were able to answer yes, the better suited you are to a career in teaching.

## Preschool Teachers

Children enter preschool (or nursery school, as it is often called) when they are three or four. They have no idea what school is like, except perhaps from playing school with older brothers and sisters or neighborhood children. Preschool teachers have the task of introducing young children to school and preparing them for kindergarten. Even though kindergarten has become more academic, preschool teachers do not directly teach young children to read, write, or do mathematics. Instead, they capitalize on children's play to further their language and vocabulary development and introduce scientific and mathematical concepts. Their major task, however, is to help children learn to get along in a classroom situation. They must be taught to listen attentively, to solve problems, to manipulate their hands effectively, to socialize with their classmates, to express themselves clearly, and to take care of their basic needs. And while the children are learning these things, the preschool teacher must fan their desire to learn through interesting activities for groups and individuals. Good preschool teachers give young children a big boost up the ladder of school success. It could be the job for you if you especially like working with young children.

If you decide to become a preschool teacher, you will be working in the fastest-growing area of education. More and more young children are now attending school earlier and earlier because both parents are working, and this number is expected to increase greatly as preschool education becomes mandatory in many states. You will be working in pleasant surroundings in converted houses, churches, new or remodeled buildings, child care centers, and public or private schools.

## Training and Education Requirements

Employment requirements vary widely for preschool teachers. Most states require a certificate to teach in a public preschool. Some require a bachelor's degree in early childhood education; others require an associate's degree; and still others require certification by a nationally recognized authority.

Preschool teachers in private schools usually face less-stringent requirements. Some enter the field through the Child Development Associate (CDA) program offered by the Council for Early Childhood Professional Recognition. The program requires a mix of classroom training and experience working with children, along with an independent assessment of an individual's competence. You can also study to become a preschool teacher through the American Montessori Society, which offers many different programs.

## A Look Inside the Preschool Classroom

Long before the first child ever enters the classroom, preschool teachers have made preparations for the day. They have created lesson plans describing what the children will do, selected story-books, mixed paints, and set up craft projects. From the minute children walk through the classroom door, the teacher is busy greeting, guiding, assisting, and encouraging each individual student as well as organizing group activities. The teacher also has to spot children who are not feeling well, listen to complaints, and comfort the sad or injured child. As a preschool teacher, you need to have an excellent understanding of children, how they develop, and what their abilities are at each age level. It is also essential for preschool teachers to have the capability of creating activities that are appropriate to individual children at various age levels.

## The Rewards of Teaching Preschool

Being a preschool teacher is immensely rewarding because your students really show their affection for you. You also have the opportunity to fuel their energy and enthusiasm for learning. As a teacher at this level, you will work relatively short hours. There is also the added bonus of having time off for all major holidays, plus a long summer vacation.

## Earnings

Your salary as a preschool teacher will probably be based upon your education level and the number of years of teaching experience you have. You may only receive an hourly wage, and it could be less than $10 per hour in a private preschool. Only preschool teachers in public schools who have state teacher certification earn salaries comparable to kindergarten and elementary school teachers, who can earn an average of more than $45,000 a year. Benefits such as health insurance and paid vacations for preschool teachers vary widely, with some schools providing good benefits and others offering no benefits at all.

## What It's Like to Be a Preschool Teacher

For more than twenty-five years, Cathy Johnson has been following a family tradition of teaching. Her mother taught at the first-grade level for forty-nine years. As she was growing up, Cathy observed her mother's love for teaching and saw the contribution to children's lives that her mother was making. To pursue her desired career as a preschool teacher, Cathy obtained a kindergarten endorsement and a master's degree in early childhood education.

Today, Cathy is a lead teacher in a preschool. She has the responsibility of selecting what will be taught in the classroom, planning how it will be taught, and teaching the lesson. In addition, Cathy has two aides who support what she is doing in the classroom. Another of her jobs is holding conferences with parents, and she writes notes letting them know how their children are doing. Lead teachers also handle all the paperwork involved in running a class.

Cathy feels that a good preschool teacher must be patient and firm with his or her young students. Yet she also believes that it is necessary to be loving and very flexible. Cathy loves her job so much that she has far more things that she likes than dislikes about her job, but here are a few things that Cathy dislikes about her job:

1. She has inadequate benefits. The teachers at her preschool do not have health or medical insurance.
2. The close-knit relationships that she forms with her preschool children vanish over the years. Five or ten years later, many do not remember Cathy when they see her on the street.
3. The job is physically demanding, as she has to bounce and jump around with the children.
4. She tends to pick up ailments as so many children come to school sick.

# Kindergarten Teachers

As a kindergarten teacher, you will be a giant in a miniature world of small tables, chairs, easels, and playthings. You will introduce young children to the world of letters and numbers, open their eyes to the joys of art and music, and help them learn about themselves and the world around them. You will pass on knowledge to a future generation of plumbers, doctors, pilots, and political leaders. As a kindergarten teacher, you will be challenged each day to provide interesting, exciting, and motivating activities that make young children want to learn. They will also be learning the most important lessons of life in their kindergarten classrooms, such as sharing, respecting others, telling the truth, and trying to do their best at all times.

As a kindergarten teacher, you will have the opportunity to be more than just their teacher; you will also be a nurse, a peacemaker for fights, a supervisor on the playground, a mother or father, and, most important of all, a friend.

## Requirements for Employment

The exact requirements for being a kindergarten teacher vary from state to state. To teach in most public school kindergartens you need to have state certification. Usually, this certificate entitles you to teach from kindergarten through sixth or eighth grade. To obtain this certificate, you need to have studied early childhood education in college and earned a bachelor's degree in education. As part of your job, you will also be expected to have a certain degree of skill in both art and music.

## A Look Inside the Kindergarten Classroom

In the past, kindergarten classes were typically half-day classes with morning or afternoon sessions. Today, 60 percent of all kindergartens are full-day programs. As a kindergarten teacher, you will typically teach all day.

The kindergarten curriculum is also changing. The focus is no longer entirely on preparing children for first grade. Because so many children have attended preschool, more attention is now being given to academic skills. This is due in part to parental pressure for more academics and to the No Child Left Behind legislation. Some kindergarten teachers are even teaching a scaled-back first grade curriculum. In fact, one in five kindergarten teachers now assigns homework. By the end of the year, your kindergarten students will probably be expected to know the sounds of all the letters and to recognize the numbers to ten. In some kindergartens, you may be expected to have them reading simple stories, writing sentences, and doing very basic math. Some teachers use worksheets to teach these skills. Most use hands-on activities to help children learn these beginning academic skills. Even though you will be presenting more academics in kindergarten, there will still be plenty of time for art, music, and physical activities.

## Earnings

Whether you teach kindergarten, first grade, middle school, or high school, your salary will be based on the degrees you hold and the number of years you have taught. There is, however, some political pressure for a merit system in which teachers are paid for their effectiveness in the classroom. According to the American Federation of Teachers, education salaries are still not competitive with other professions. The average teacher salary is now more than $45,000 per year. Beginning teachers, depending on where they work, earn between $23,700 and $38,600. Public school teachers typically have benefit packages that include health insurance and life insurance. Furthermore, teachers receive a specified amount of paid sick leave, and some school districts also allow one or more days for conducting personal business. Many public school teachers belong to unions that bargain with the school district over wages, hours, and other conditions of employment such as class size and payment for directing extracurricular activities.

## What It's Like to Be a Kindergarten Teacher

Jackie McVey has been teaching kindergarten for several years. She first became interested in a teaching career after being a Sunday school teacher and returned to college to become a kindergarten teacher.

Jackie teaches at a cooperative kindergarten, which is a school operated by parents. The parents of her students take turns acting as aides in the classroom, which gives her two aides to help at all times. Not only does she have the opportunity to meet her students' parents, but many of their grandparents often assist her as well. At the end of the year, Jackie throws a slumber party with twelve hours of playing games and movies. This year ten parents came to the overnight party.

A cooperative school is really a family school. Families act as resource people who suggest interesting activities for the class. One year, Jackie's class went to a pro-football locker room and even had the chance to try on pads because one of the fathers was a professional football player. Another father who was chairman of a parade took the children to see the floats being built.

As a kindergarten teacher, Jackie feels that she has an abundance of happy moments. Every day the children give her warm hugs and friendly smiles. She is thrilled when a struggling student finally succeeds in performing a task. Jackie points out that a kindergarten teacher needs to like not only working with children but also dealing with parents. The relationship between parents and teachers at this level is very important in helping young children do well in school.

# Elementary Teachers

If you are not enthusiastic about having to tie shoes, wipe noses, and button coats for preschoolers and kindergartners, you might find it more enjoyable to teach in the elementary grades. Teachers at this level usually don't have to handle many of the children's personal needs. Rather, they are focused on helping students become independent learners. Besides classes in reading and mathematics, elementary students are beginning to learn in the content areas of history, science, health, and English. You will be helping children to expand their horizons.

## Employment Requirements

Every state requires public elementary school teachers to be certified. In general, certification requirements include a college degree and the completion of an approved teacher training program. Plus, most states require continuing education for renewal of the teacher's license. More and more states are now moving toward requiring teachers to pass a rigorous comprehensive teaching examination to obtain a provisional license and then to demonstrate satisfactory teaching performance over an extended period of time to obtain full licensure. Also, in most states you will have to pass a competency test demonstrating that you have certain basic skills, and many school districts require additional testing before you can enter the classroom.

## On the Job

Elementary teachers typically have one class of children to whom they teach several subjects a day. There may be special teachers who take students for music, art, gym, and library time. Teachers are kept busy all day because they frequently have to supervise lunchrooms, recesses, and bus loading.

Elementary school teachers plan lessons, prepare tests, grade papers, make out report cards, meet with parents, and attend faculty meetings and conferences. They also assign lessons, give tests, hear oral presentations, and oversee special projects. Teachers also have the job of keeping order in their classrooms and diagnosing and correcting learning problems.

Elementary school teachers must be:

- disciplinarians, making sure that the children follow the set rules
- team players, working with the other teachers and staff members in the school building
- communications experts, expressing orally and in writing to parents and other educators how well the children in their classes are performing
- listeners, hearing what the children are saying about their problems
- referees, solving problems that occur between students
- motivators, encouraging students to want to acquire knowledge
- performers, grabbing and keeping the attention of students as they teach each lesson throughout the day
- secretaries, keeping records, filling out forms, and completing reports
- jacks-of-all-trades, having to teach music, art, physical education, and other subjects beyond the basics
- lunchroom or playground monitors, making sure that everyone is orderly
- computer experts, researching lessons, keeping records, and teaching students how to use computers

## The Rewards

Being an elementary school teacher is a great job if you love being around children all day. You will see how your lessons are motivating young children to learn. And there is so much delight in observing how the students in your classroom are developing and learning during the year you spend with them. You are an active participant in teaching children the basic skills they will need throughout their lives.

## Earnings

As an elementary school teacher in a public school, your salary and benefits will be the same as those of public school kindergarten teachers. Contact your state's department of education to find out what the salary range is for teachers in your state. You will usually earn less if you elect to work in a private school.

## What It's Like to Be an Elementary Teacher

Susan Lawton is a second grade teacher in a large public school system. She comes from a family of teachers. Her mother was a teacher, as well as her great aunt and both of her older sisters. Susan got an early start in her profession when she worked in a school laboratory at a nursery school during college. She was able to observe the teacher daily and interact with the children. Susan feels that teaching was a wise career choice for her. In fact, she can't think of any other career that better suits her, as she enjoys being wanted, needed, and useful.

Susan especially likes the start of each school year, getting to see former students and meeting new children. The first day of school in her lesson plan book looks like this:

### LESSON PLAN FOR GRADE 2

- 9:20 A.M.—1st Bell. Students enter and find own desk and chair. Encourage them to become acquainted with school materials on desks (folder, pencils, crayons). Morning work: answer student questionnaire on favorite things.
- 9:30 A.M.—2nd Bell. Opening activities: take attendance, collect lunch money and parent notes, say pledge. Discuss how to listen to announcements each morning.
- 9:45 A.M.—"Get acquainted" at big circle:
  1. Discuss bulletin board with teacher's favorite things.
  2. Introduce the "Star Student" bulletin board.
  3. Have children talk about summer vacations.

- 10:00 A.M.—Children do summer vacation drawing project at their desks.
- 10:30 A.M.—Discussion of classroom rules:
  1. Proper handling of classroom objects.
  2. Usage of restroom passes.
  3. Consequences for breaking rules.
- 10:45 A.M.—Take class restroom break.
- 11:00 A.M.—Tour school building:
  1. Show special classrooms (art, music, gym, library, computer room), cafeteria, school office, teacher's mailbox.
  2. Introduce principal and secretary.
- 11:30 A.M.—Class discussion:
  1. Discuss homework policy.
  2. Suggest study habits for home.
  3. Recommend homework kit (markers, ruler, paper, pencils) and keeping a box for storing each grading period's work.
  4. Explain grading system.
  5. Give tips on how to be successful in second grade.
- 12:00 P.M.—Discuss lunch and recess procedures.
- 12:15 P.M.—Lunch and 12:45 recess.
- 1:20 P.M.—Restroom break.
- 1:30 P.M.—Story time.
- 1:45 P.M.—"Me Project." Construct personalized cubes using magazines to find pictures of favorite items, hobbies, sports, and so on to glue on cubes. (Pass out glue, scissors, cubes).
- 2:30 P.M.—Distribute textbooks and show class how to organize them in desks with morning books on the left, afternoon books on the right.
- 3:00 P.M.—Go over how papers are to be headed. Pass out lined paper. Practice writing first and last names, teacher's name, and school. Write sentences together about first school day.

- 3:30 P.M.—Free play. Allow children time to familiarize themselves with classroom games and socialize with new and old school friends.
- 3:50 P.M.—Discuss cleaning-up procedures and then clean up.
- 3:55 P.M.—Discuss dismissal procedures and listen to day-end announcements.
- 4:00 P.M.—Announcements.
- 4:05 P.M.—1st Bell. Bus students leave with patrol person.
- 4:10 P.M.—2nd Bell. Walkers and riders follow patrol person. Prepare next day's morning work (school word search). Put stickers on incentive charts for those who earned them.
- 4:20 P.M.—Pull shades and close door.

Susan feels that her happiest moments in teaching come when her students from previous years return and tell her what a great teacher they thought she was or what they remember about being in her classroom. She finds it fascinating to see what they have done with their lives and what careers they have chosen. And it is satisfying to Susan to know that she can take credit for some of her former students' successes.

# Middle School Teachers

If you want the challenge of working with children as they are starting to cross the bridge to adolescence and you would enjoy spending most of your day teaching one subject, then a teaching position in middle school is for you. Teachers at this grade level can climb the career ladder to become department heads. As a department head, you would be responsible for all the teachers teaching the same general subject, such as English, math, or science. You would work with the teachers to decide what is to be taught in each class and help them with any problems. And you also might be involved in rating the teachers' performances.

## On the Job

As a middle school teacher, you are able to teach a specialized subject area that truly interests you. You write lesson plans for each class, make and correct tests, collect homework, and contact parents when it is necessary. Also, you are required to perform routine bookkeeping tasks, such as taking attendance for every class. Usually you give lectures on a specific topic and expect your students to take notes. You do not provide answers for every question at this level but rather encourage your students to seek out the information for themselves. Your day will probably be divided into six to eight periods, with a free period to prepare for your classes. Also, it is likely that you will work with students in school-sponsored activities.

## The Rewards

It is a pleasure to be able to teach one subject that you truly enjoy all day long. And it is delightful to see how much your students change and grow up during the school year and to be part of helping them become more mature.

## What It's Like to Be a Middle School Teacher

Titus Exum was taught in school that education is the key to success. While graduation from high school was an accomplishment, he knew that a college degree would open the door to earnings that high school graduates and dropouts could never experience. Teachers pushed this message home to him. Today, Titus gives his eighth grade American history students the same message.

Titus has a bachelor's degree in elementary education and a master's degree in school administration and supervision. He holds elementary credentials in Missouri and Alaska. To obtain his present job, Titus had to take the National Teacher Examination.

Titus works as part of a five-person teaching team. Each teacher teaches only one subject; however, they work together to plan assemblies, arrange field trips, discuss student behavior problems, select guest speakers, and handle other situations involving all of the eighth grade teachers. He finds that the hardest part of his job is motivating those students who are not interested in learning history. Many of these students have discovered early in their schooling that they will be passed on to the next grade regardless of their academic efforts.

Titus feels that he has had a successful day when the students in his five classes actively participate in a class or group project, a class discussion, or a multilevel assignment. Then he can see the students actually learning in his classes.

# Elementary Teachers of Specific Subjects

You might decide that you want to teach a specific subject in elementary school. For example, most elementary schools have reading teachers, music teachers, and physical education teachers on their teaching staffs. If you decide to become one of these teachers, you will need to study this area in depth in college as well as meet requirements for a teaching certificate in your area.

## What It's Like to Be a Music Teacher

Teaching music is an excellent way to share a love of music with children, from fledgling musicians in preschool to skilled graduate students in a university. Since each age level offers different challenges and rewards, prospective music teachers need to decide which age group most appeals to them. At all levels, music teachers in schools have a number of duties that must be performed, from taking attendance to giving grades. In addition, there are frequently state or district guidelines that prescribe the curriculum that is to be taught in music classes. Besides normal teaching duties, most music teachers usually spend time before and after school working with different musical groups or preparing students for special contests and performances.

Julia Scherer has taught music at the same elementary school for more than twenty-five years. She graduated from college with a bachelor's degree in music education. Julia had some difficulty finding a permanent job right after college, but while applying for a substitute teacher position she discovered that the district was looking for a music teacher. Julia applied for the job and was hired. Like most music teachers, Julia also obtained a master's degree in music and has taken additional courses. As an elementary music specialist, Julia teaches general music classes, which feature instruction in vocal music, composers, music reading, instruments of the orchestra, music appreciation, and playing the recorder.

## Special Education Teachers

Special education teachers work with the learning disabled, seeing and hearing impaired, and those with mental, physical, and emotional disabilities. They work closely with doctors, social workers, psychologists, speech pathologists, and parents to make sure that each child's Individual Education Plan (IEP) is helping the child learn to the best of his or her ability. Special education teachers may not always be working in a school setting; they might work at an institution or a residential center. They might even live with their students or be required to visit in their homes.

Special education teachers must earn a bachelor's degree, complete an approved teacher preparation program, and hold a special education license. Many states even require a master's degree. At the present time, there are excellent job prospects, as federal and state legislation requires schools to provide more special education programs. Salaries for special education teachers follow the same pay scale as that for general education teachers.

### What It's Like to Be a Special Education Teacher

While JoAnn Finch-Martin was in high school, she started babysitting and soon realized that she wanted a career that would allow her to work with children. After taking a child development class and working as a volunteer at a shelter, she knew that her career would involve working with special-needs children. Today, JoAnn works with just six young students in her classroom. Because of their disabilities (autism, Down's syndrome, cerebral palsy, and moderate mental retardation), she has two classroom aides.

JoAnn's day begins when she helps four of her students eat breakfast in the school cafeteria. She helps two of them open their eating utensils and food packs. Learning to handle this task is part of the students' formal goals—acquisition of fine motor manipulation skills. Breakfast only lasts for about twenty-four minutes, but it is a hectic time, with JoAnn always on her feet helping the four students.

The day continues in the classroom, where the students hang up their coats, take down the chairs, and then go to the restroom to wash their faces and hands and take care of any other toileting needs. The daily routine begins with the saying of the pledge of allegiance, followed by the morning circle. During this time, the students participate in a variety of activities, from calendar reading and counting the days on the calendar to drilling on colors, shapes, and the alphabet. Both JoAnn and the aides encourage the children for the slightest participation.

After morning circle, the students take a quick restroom break. Two of the children have goals to improve their toileting skills, which require the attention of JoAnn and the aides. During the snack break that follows, all of the children are helped to work on their eating goals.

After snack time, the children clean the table, push the chairs in, and sweep the floor. Then they join together on the carpet to do their morning exercises, which are followed by time at the gadget center, where the children work on such tasks as sorting colors and making chains from links. The morning ends with the children choosing a special activity. Although this time is called recreation and leisure time, there is really no leisure for JoAnn and her aids, as each child needs constant individual attention.

JoAnn has a challenging job because her students have multiple disabilities, and her lesson plans must be individualized. She can have a central theme, but each child's plan must be structured for his or her special needs.

..............

# Tutors

Tutors work one-on-one with children to help them acquire the skills needed to do well in school. Elementary school tutors usually concentrate on helping children acquire basic skills in reading, writing, and mathematics and also spend considerable time teaching study skills. High school tutors typically work with a student on a single subject, such as calculus or Spanish. While elementary school tutors have usually taught in a classroom, high school tutors may only have special expertise in a subject.

Some tutors work in learning centers; however, most tutors either set up businesses in their own homes or go to the homes of individual students. Tutors running their own businesses usually need to invest in a wide range of curriculum materials in order to help their individual clients.

If you decide on a career as a tutor, you should expect to work afternoons, evenings, and weekends when children are not in school. Most tutors work part-time, although it is possible to have a full-time career as a tutor. What you earn as a tutor depends on the number of clients you have, your expertise, and the area where you live. Tutors can expect to earn between fifteen and fifty dollars an hour. A tutor with unusual expertise might command as much as seventy-five dollars an hour.

## What It's Like to Be a Tutor

Pennie Needham brings exceptional qualifications to her job as a tutor. Not only has she taught in classrooms from elementary school through college, she also has special education credentials that attest to her skills in diagnosing the educational problems of her clients. When clients are referred to her, Pennie begins by giving diagnostic tests to pinpoint exactly what the child's weaknesses and strengths are. Then she holds a conference with the parents to set up a plan to help the child. She works with each client for only one hour a week; however, it is more than an hour's work for Pennie because she has to prepare work for each session as well as communicate with parents and teachers about how the child is progressing. Pennie schedules her clients after school during the week. In the summer, they can visit earlier in the day. She finds being a tutor a very satisfying career because she is really helping children. The best part is seeing a client do so well in school that the child no longer needs her services. Pennie advises prospective tutors to investigate this career while still in school by serving as peer tutors to classmates.

## Other Jobs in Education

The focus of this chapter is on classroom teaching. Some teachers climb the career ladder and become curriculum directors, assistant principals, principals, assistant superintendents, and superintendents. These professionals still work for the welfare of children but are no longer directly involved with them. At every school, there are jobs other than teaching that let you work directly with children. Counselors work with one child at a time or with small groups of children. And school secretaries and lunchroom employees spend much of their workdays with children.

## Your Future in Teaching

As a teacher of children of any age, you help to shape a future generation. You are a very important person in the life of every one of your students. As a teacher, you are constantly challenged to find new and innovative techniques to motivate each child to learn in his or her special way. You also have to handle a wide variety of supercharged emotions, from helping a young child adjust to being away from home for the first time to getting a hyperactive child to stay in his or her seat. You are involved in a job that is rewarding, challenging, and hectic but never boring. And you should not have much trouble finding a job, as teaching positions are expected to be abundant in most areas in the next ten years.

# CHAPTER SEVEN

# Sports and Recreation Careers

*Definition: A sports and recreation worker gives children the opportunity to learn new skills and participate in enjoyable free-time activities.*

We spend much of our leisure time participating in activities such as playing tennis, swimming, golfing, hiking, camping, and boating. What could be more appealing to kids at heart than a career teaching children a sport or helping them enjoy their recreation time? These careers truly present the opportunity to combine avocation and vocation. Avid golfers who adore children may spend their workdays helping children master the intricacies of the sport. Former world-class karate champions can see their coaching efforts produce junior champions. Camp counselors can share their love of the outdoors with children as they canoe down small streams together or hike through the woods. When you work with children in sports and recreation careers, the children are enthusiastic and eager to learn a new skill or share an enjoyable activity with you.

## Careers in Sports

If you enjoy working with children and have a passion for a particular sport, you will be able to find work wherever there are a large number of children and the appropriate sports facilities.

Almost all children enjoy sports. Besides watching and talking about sports, children want to be skilled athletes. To accomplish this goal, they need the help of experienced instructors. As a sports instructor, you have the opportunity to teach eager children swimming, gymnastics, tennis, golf, bowling, bicycling, basketball, baseball, horseback riding, archery, badminton, ice hockey, soccer, scuba diving, fencing, and every other imaginable sport. Parents want their children to have these skills, and children dream of being future Michael Jordans and Michelle Kwans. This desire to excel in a sport often continues through high school as children work to attract the attention of a college or professional sports recruiter.

## On the Job as a Sports Instructor

Many careers as sports instructors involve working both with children and adults. For example, while children are in school, a tennis instructor might give lessons to adults. However, gymnastics instructors work almost entirely with children. Until school is out, they work with preschool children. Then they will work late into the evening with school-age gymnasts. Part of a sports instructor's job is the supervision of the children in the facility when they are not receiving instruction. And in some sports, the instructor is responsible for keeping the equipment in tip-top shape.

## What Is Involved in Teaching a Sport

Most sports instructors have actively played in the sports they teach. Often, they have reached a high level of expertise in that sport. But sports instructors must also develop teaching skills. This can be done by attending classes and workshops given by sports associations and colleges. Sports instructors can keep their skills updated by reading magazines, books, and newsletters in their sports areas. Certification is important for sports instructors as it shows their knowledge of a sport. Requirements usually include being eighteen years old and certified in CPR, although that will vary with the sports organization. Many require participation in a clinic, camp, or school for certification. Besides knowing teaching techniques and having a genuine affection for children, sports instructors need to have the following aptitudes to work successfully with children:

- an understanding of how each student learns most effectively
- the ability to communicate with children and their parents
- an ability to share their personal enthusiasm for a sport
- the capability of teaching a sport to children who are destined to be champions as well as to those with limited talents
- a good sense of humor
- the ability to make drills, practice sessions, and lessons enjoyable for children
- good organizational skills
- a strong sense of ethics
- high moral standards
- an ability to treat all children fairly
- the ability to handle children's emotional outbursts
- the ability to build children's self-esteem
- the ability to help children develop confidence in their own abilities
- a high energy level

## Advantages and Disadvantages of a Sports Instruction Career

Like all careers, sports instruction has both advantages and disadvantages. Let's explore the advantages first:

- being appreciated by your students
- considerable freedom, if not total freedom, in determining how you teach
- being your own boss in many cases

- having a profession that is also your number one avocation
- wearing comfortable sports apparel on the job
- exercising on the job, which promotes good health
- having a job that changes with each child or group of children and may also vary with the season

The following list explores some of the disadvantages associated with working as a sports teacher:

- parents who interfere in the relationship between teacher and child
- parents who contradict your instructions
- parents who do not appreciate the importance of sports
- having work hours that are the opposite of your own children's time away from school

## Job Outlook and Earnings

Employment of sports instructors for children is expected to grow about as fast as the average of all occupations. It is fueled by the desire of parents to help their children gain sports skills so they can make high school and college teams and possibly have careers as professional athletes. Plus, parents value the health benefits of their children being actively engaged in a sport.

Earnings vary considerably for sports instructors depending upon their reputations, the facilities where they work, and geographic regions. Some instructors receive a salary, while others may be paid by the hour, per session, or by the number of participants. The average income of sports instructors is less than $25,000 per year. However, giving private lessons is a popular way to increase income.

## What It's Like to Be a Tennis Pro

P. A. Nilhagen was an excellent junior tennis player. He gave his first tennis lesson in Sweden when he was only sixteen and earned six Swedish crowns (about seventy-five cents). By the time he finished high school, P.A. had only one goal—to be a teaching pro. Today, he is the director of junior development for one of the largest tennis programs in the United States.

P.A. was ranked in the top ten of Sweden's junior division when he was seventeen and eighteen. He was a member of the Swedish Junior Davis Cup Team. His tennis accomplishments led to a college scholarship in the United States. For four years, he played tennis at Western Kentucky University. P.A. underwent special training in order to become a tennis pro. In Sweden he took training courses to gain certification, and in the United States he is certified by the U.S. Professional Tennis Association (USPTA). At Western Kentucky University, he earned a bachelor's degree in physical education. Today, he continues his tennis education by regularly attending the USPTA's teachers' conference held in New York City during the U.S. Open, as well as several other USPTA-sponsored conventions. He subscribes to eight tennis magazines and reads every available tennis book to learn more about the sport. Also, P.A. has videotapes to study of every televised tennis match since 1981.

P.A.'s first job was as a pro at a very large Midwestern tennis facility. After only a few months, he became head pro and shortly thereafter director of the club's junior development program. P.A. is the only coach in the Midwest to remain at one club for more than thirty years. For the greater part of the year, he teaches tennis in the club's indoor facilities. When summer comes, he is outdoors running one of the largest youth tennis programs in the nation.

P.A.'s daily schedule usually looks like this:

- 5 A.M.—P.A. gets up and eats a healthy breakfast.
- 7 A.M.—He arrives at work one hour before his first lesson to prepare for the day.
- 7 A.M. to 5 P.M.—He is in charge of the on-court activities, which include group lessons, private instruction, and challenge matches.
- 5 P.M. to 7 P.M.—He spends time in parent or player meetings.

Even though it is late, P.A.'s day is not over yet, as he often spends another hour or two talking on the phone with players discussing strategies and approaching matches. As you can see, a tennis pro does not always work a forty-hour week.

P.A. believes a teacher must do his or her best with every student. He is motivated to find different things in each child's game so that lessons will never be boring for him or for the student he is teaching. P.A. is never late for a lesson, as he respects his students too much to be late. He sees himself doing the same job five years from now—only better because he will have five more years of experience.

Some of P.A.'s happiest moments on the job have been when his students have won state, western, national, or professional titles. He especially remembers being at Wimbledon with Todd Witsken and watching as his stepson won the state doubles championship.

P.A.'s advice to prospective teachers or coaches of any sport is to make sure that you love your sport and the people you will be training in that sport. He also suggests finding a role model whom you can emulate. Finally, P.A. believes that sports teachers should stay fit and dress professionally.

## What It's Like to Run a Gymnastics Studio

Terry Spencer's talent for gymnastics was discovered early on. When she was five, a master gymnast and teacher asked her to join his team. By six, Terry told her mother that she was going to the Olympics, and she almost did. She was a member of the 1968 Olympic team but had to leave the squad because of a sprained ankle. And while working out for the 1972 Olympic Games, she took a terrible fall. Everyone thought her back was broken. At that moment, Terry, not knowing if she would ever walk again, decided that she would teach the sport she loved from a wheelchair if her competitive career was over. Fortunately, Terry's back was not broken, and she was able to end her career in a burst of glory at the 1973 World University Games in Moscow, where she competed against Olympic gold medalist Olga Korbut. Terry finished at the highest level for a female gymnast from the United States.

After her competitive gymnastics career was over, Terry briefly promoted gymnastics for the owner of several gymnastics camps before opening her own studio. When Terry first started her studio, she worked from ten in the morning until one in the afternoon, then returned to the gym at four and stayed until ten at night. Today, her World of Gymnastics studio has a staff of thirteen and more than five hundred students attending classes for fun and at ten different team competition levels. The studio is open six days a week. On Sundays, the coaches take students to meets, or meets are hosted at the studio. Terry's efficient staff has allowed her to trim her teaching hours to between 4 P.M. and 10 P.M. She reserves mornings for doing paperwork at home while other staffers teach preschool sessions. She has given up coaching; however, she still teaches young children. Terry is now in her fourteenth year as the very successful operator of a gymnastics studio.

She lives for the hugs that appreciative children shower upon her. Terry's happiest moments on the job come when her gymnastic teams do well in competition, as she has helped them reach this skill level. On the downside, she finds it difficult to deal with parents who expect too much from their children, as well as with those parents who do not believe their children have any potential. Nevertheless, she manages to deal with the parents because she cares so much about teaching children gymnastics.

Terry points out that being the owner of a gym requires one special aptitude—stamina. She must have the strength to handle the staff, parents, children, and herself, along with all the problems that come with running a studio. She feels that the most difficult thing about owning her own studio is all the paperwork involved in operating a business, from collecting money and paying rent to buying insurance. None of this work, however, detracts from her pride in owning a thriving gymnastics studio.

Terry loves gymnastics and cares about educating children in its intricacies. She enjoys teaching young children from the beginning the right way to perform a move in case they wish to become serious gymnasts later on. And she never pushes children until they have built up their own confidence.

# Careers in Recreation

Children do not automatically know how to make meaningful and creative use of their leisure time. For too many children, leisure time means sitting in front of a television set and passively absorbing what is happening on the screen. Professionals in recreation enhance children's lives by showing them ways to use their leisure time more productively and enjoyably. You will find recreation jobs in such places as community recreation and parks departments, the YMCA and YWCA, scouting and similar programs, and summer camps. There are also jobs at amusement parks, hotels and resorts, tourist attractions, and wilderness and survival enterprises. You could find yourself operating a ride at an amusement park, or you might be leading a recreation program in which you direct the activities in a community park. Unfortunately, many of these jobs are only part-time or summer jobs.

## Training for Recreation Careers

To have a successful career in many areas of recreation, you need to be a teacher, a planner, an organizer, and a motivator. And for many jobs you must have a specific competency. For example, camp counselors are often expected to teach skills ranging from archery to horseback riding. Full-time professionals in recreation are increasingly obtaining degrees in recreation from two- or four-year college programs. Besides courses in recreation, they take classes in psychology, sociology, communications, and the performing arts.

While you can get a job as a recreation worker with just a high school diploma, you are not likely to advance to a supervisor or higher-level administrative job without a bachelor's degree. In fact, many recreation workers are now getting master's degrees in recreation or related areas in order to climb the career ladder in this field. Another advantage to getting formal training in recreation is that it gives you an edge in the keen competition for full-time jobs. It is much easier to get a part-time job without specific training.

Besides education, certification can be an asset to your career in recreation. The National Recreation and Park Association offers certification both to individuals with college degrees in recreation and to those who have less than four years of college education. There are three levels of certification based on education and experience: Certified Park and Recreation Professional, Provisional Park and Recreation Professional, and Associate Park and Recreation Professional.

## Job Outlook and Earnings

Employment of full-time recreation workers is expected to grow faster than the average of all occupations. Unfortunately, when you choose a career as a full-time recreation worker, you can expect to earn significantly less than the average for workers in all other occupations.

If you are among the 40 percent of workers employed by local governments, you will earn close to nine dollars per hour. Your pay will be less if you are employed by a civic or social organization such as the Boy or Girl Scouts or the Red Cross. Only recreation directors and others in supervisory positions can earn significantly more than the average. If you work full-time for either a public or a private agency, you will receive typical benefits. On the other hand, part-time workers receive few, if any, benefits.

## What It's Like to Be a YMCA Program Director

Jennifer O'Leary's involvement with the YMCA began during college when she worked summers at a day camp. At first, Jennifer was a counselor at the day camp, responsible for all the activities of a group of ten to twelve children ranging in age from first to fifth grade. She helped the children learn how to cook and do crafts and played sports and games with them. When the group went away from the camp to swim, she had to make sure that the children returned with all of their belongings. One day a week, the campers went on field trips to water parks, museums, zoos, or other attractions, and Jennifer was responsible for her group for the entire day. While the camp was from 8:30 A.M. to 4:30 P.M., she actually worked longer as she had to spend additional time working in the extended day-care program.

After two summers of working as a counselor, Jennifer became the on-site director of the camp. She not only served as a counselor of a small group of children but also had the responsibility of overseeing the rest of the staff and planning all the activities. Jennifer had gained the experience to handle this job by watching the director and stepping in when the director wasn't there.

Besides her experience at day camp, Jennifer had also worked part-time in an on-site Y child care program while she was in college. After graduation, she worked part-time at the Y in her hometown and was soon offered a position as the full-time director of a new after-school child care facility. Jennifer was able to get this job because she had so much experience working in Y programs and had taken an early childhood administration class that was essential for this position. In this job, she spent most of her time planning activities and working with the children plus hiring and supervising the staff.

After serving as a facility director for two years, Jennifer became a program director responsible for two child care programs, a family camp, the Papoose program for fathers and preschoolers, and six summer camps. Although she supervises all these programs, she still gets to work with children, especially at summer day camp. Jennifer is one kid at heart who has been successful in finding a satisfying career working with children. In the future, she may open her own home day-care center.

## What It's Like to Climb the YMCA Career Ladder

Thom Martin has been been involved with the YMCA as a participant in activities, a volunteer, and a paid professional. His first involvement with the Y began when he was eight months old and in the Y's parent/infant swim program. In high school, Thom was a volunteer and a paid employee. He served as a swim instructor, day camp counselor, lifeguard, movement education instructor, and youth sports coach. During college, Thom was an assistant in a teen program during the school year and a pool manager and day-care director in the summer.

When Thom graduated from college, his first job was as a YMCA program director. He is a testimony to how working at an organization while in school can lead directly to a salaried professional job. As program director, Thom created and implemented programs, hired people to run programs, worked with volunteers, handled a budget, and supervised the programs under their auspices. Today, he is one of the youngest executive directors of a Y program and is responsible for all the activities at the facility.

Thom explains that being with the Y has let him be a part of special moments in children's lives. He is proud, too, of the positive impact that such Y programs as drug prevention have on the lives of young people. Another plus to working at the Y is that young professionals are given added responsibilities far earlier than in many other management positions. Thom describes his coworkers as great people who are family oriented. And, of course, a career at the Y is a perfect job for kids at heart because so much of the Y program is dedicated to working with children.

## What It's Like to Be a Recreation Worker

Several years ago, Laurie Archuleta Jerge was selected to receive the Robert W. Crawford Young Professional Award by the National Recreation and Park Association. The award is presented annually to those in the field who exemplify the qualities of Crawford's singularly innovative and pioneering leadership in the planning, development, and programming of a wide variety of creative community leisure opportunities and activities.

As the award demonstrates, Laurie is an outstanding recreation worker. Her career in recreation began when she was only sixteen years old after her aunt told her about a new fitness craze called aerobics. With her endless energy and enthusiasm, Laurie was a natural as an aerobics instructor. To prepare for a future career in recreation, Laurie earned a bachelor's degree in leisure recreation and a master's in human performance and sport. She is an advocate for professional certification and is a Certified Leisure Professional. She also holds such certifications as Aerobics Fitness Leader, Pool Operator, and Instructor for Red Cross CPR and First Aid, to name just a few of her many certifications.

During college, Laurie and her husband, John, owned and operated their own aerobics dance agency to help put themselves through school. Upon graduation, Laurie became the program director for a YMCA and, at the same time, a part-time instructor in the college's health, physical education, and recreation department. When the YMCA closed, she became the public relations analyst in the Roswell, New Mexico, recreation department.

Through her work in this job to educate and inform the public on the benefits of recreation, Laurie is known as the "voice of Roswell Recreation." She hosts a television program titled "Leisure Living," regularly provides information and public service announcements to the local newspaper and radio stations, gives a daily recreation report on a local radio station, and speaks to civic clubs on the benefits of parks and recreation.

Laurie is especially interested in events that focus on the family because she believes that they promote family participation and interaction and the development of family values. The recreation department believes that the employees are there to save lives, to prevent incarcerations, and to provide opportunities for people to come together. Laurie finds her job in recreation rewarding because it ties together so many different types of careers. In her work, she performs mass communications, television broadcasting, journalism, special-event productions, budget analysis, family intervention through recreational programming, safety training and prevention, and business management. Work is rarely boring for this kid at heart who helps so many families through her job.

# Working at Summer Camps

Imagine being able to ride horseback and sing around campfires while you toast marshmallows. Camp staff from counselors to directors do all of these things, as well as comfort homesick campers, help children learn to get along with each other, and supervise groups of campers. The program staff teaches skills to the children, division heads supervise several counselors, and the director is responsible for the entire camp. Most jobs for program staff, camp counselors, and division heads are part-time, whether it is a day camp or an overnight camp. Only the director is employed all year. Salaries for directors range from $15,000 to $50,000, depending on the size of the camp.

## What It Takes to Be a Camp Counselor

Camps certainly want to hire individuals who adore children, but they also want counselors who have had a year or more of college and some experience working with children as volunteers or in paid positions. In addition, counselors should demonstrate the following aptitudes:

- good judgment
- initiative and creativity
- emotional stability

- high moral character
- good health and physical stamina
- good rapport with children

## What It's Like to Be a Camp Counselor

Teenagers can start preparing themselves to be camp counselors by working as junior counselors or counselors in training when they are thirteen or fourteen. Melissa Schwartzman learned about counseling by attending day and overnight summer camps starting when she was seven years old. She really enjoyed the camaraderie of living with a group and participating in interesting activities together.

After one year of college, Melissa became a counselor at an overnight camp located in the mountains. She lived in a cabin with twelve-year-old girls and worked from 7 A.M. to 9 P.M., supervising their activities. One of her jobs was to make sure that everyone in her group participated in the activities. She would join the girls in their activities, from karate to modern dance, working to assure that everyone had a good time. Melissa also served as a friend and an away-from-home mother for the girls. Part of her job consisted of counseling the girls on relationships with each other and helping them resolve any problems that arose.

**Assistant Division Head.** After one summer as a general counselor, Melissa climbed the career ladder at her camp to become an assistant division head. There were eight division heads at the camp. Each division was responsible for a specific group of campers and had both a division head and an assistant. Melissa's group was the only coed division.

As assistant division head, she was in charge of creating the evening programs, arranging the counselor's on-duty and off-day schedules, and assigning both children and counselors to activities in her division. Melissa also had to handle many of the campers' problems that the counselors in her division couldn't resolve. She often worked closely with the camp's director to solve difficult problems. And, when necessary, she filled in for counselors.

**Division Head.** Melissa worked closely with the head of her division, who largely handled the same tasks she did. The difference between their jobs was that the division head had the ultimate responsibility for all the programs and scheduling as well as resolving the more serious disciplinary problems.

**Camp Director.** At Melissa's camp, like most other camps, the only year-round job is camp director. During the summer, the director is responsible for every aspect of the camp, from handling the campers and counselors to handling the business duties. When necessary, directors may even have to step in and repair equipment and facilities.

For the rest of the year, directors publicize the camp, prepare the program for the following year, and hire personnel for the next summer session. Some directors will, however, work at camps year-round, for some camps are open on weekends for campers.

## Finding a Job at a Camp

You can find leads to job opportunities at churches, scouting organizations, and the YMCA and YWCA. Job competition is fierce because of the recreational aspects of this job as well as the opportunity to work with children. Having special qualifications, such as lifeguard or first aid or CPR certification, is helpful in finding a job. The *Guide to Accredited Camps* has summer job information as well as professional development course information. It can be obtained by contacting:

American Camping Association
5000 State Road 67 North
Martinsville, IN 46151
www.acacamps.org

# The Enjoyment of a Career in Sports and Recreation

The greatest benefit of having a career working with children in sports and recreation is being able to share the love you have for an activity with children. They truly like learning new skills and interesting ways to use their leisure time. Sports instructors have the pleasure of teaching children a cherished skill, while recreation specialists enjoy helping children learn fun and healthy ways to use their leisure time.

# CHAPTER EIGHT

# Children's Health Careers

*Definition: Children's health workers help sick children become well and help healthy children stay that way.*

Healthy children are happy and ready to learn about the world, enjoy their families and friends, play games, participate in sports, and even do chores. At no time in history have so many people worked in careers devoted to improving the health of children. When we think of keeping children healthy, our first thoughts are often of pediatricians and family practitioners. While they are valued health care professionals, many others work diligently in the health care arena to ensure that children are healthy. These include pediatric specialists, nurses and nurse practitioners, those involved in pediatric dentistry, the staff of pediatric wards and children's hospitals, speech-language pathologists, as well as all the psychiatrists, psychologists, and counselors helping ill or troubled children. A veritable army of compassionate individuals chose these careers because they want to help children, and the demand for these professionals continues to expand. You will find them working in private practices, group practices, hospitals, and clinics.

## Working in Pediatric Medicine

Pediatric medicine deals with childhood diseases and the care of infants and children in health and sickness. Pediatrics did not become a medical specialty in the United States until shortly before the Civil War, when Dr. Abraham Jacobi established the first children's clinic in New York City. It was not until 1880 that a pediatric section was organized within the American Medical Association and the medical profession recognized that children were not simply small adults.

Much of the knowledge about the treatment of children has emerged since the turn of the century. Many serious diseases that were once considered fatal can now be treated successfully, so the emphasis in pediatrics has shifted toward prevention of illness. Furthermore, it is now recognized that each child has unique needs and special characteristics that must be considered in helping the child develop into a healthy adult.

As more became known about the health needs of children, a number of pediatric specialties evolved. The variety is truly mind-boggling. Consider all the areas in which those who want to work with children in health care can find jobs:

- adolescent medicine
- allergies
- audiology
- bronchopulmonary medicine
- cardiology
- craniofacial anomalies
- counseling
- dentistry
- dermatology
- diabetes
- eating disorders
- endocrinology
- gastroenterology and nutrition
- genetics
- hematology
- infant development
- infectious diseases

- metabolics
- neonatonology
- neurogenetics
- neurology
- obesity
- oncology
- opthalmology
- orthopedics
- primary care
- psychiatry
- psychology
- research
- rheumatology
- speech-language pathology
- spina bifida
- surgery
- urology

# Exploring Medical Careers

As you have seen, career possibilities within the medical field are wide open. Specific training is necessary for almost every career. There are vocational school and community college programs for those who wish to be technicians. However, most medical careers require a college degree. And for some professions, postgraduate education following college plus additional years of internship and residency training are necessary. Furthermore, entry into postgraduate programs is very selective. Successful candidates must demonstrate academic excellence and have high scores on graduate school admissions tests.

## The Demand for Medical Personnel

There are definitely jobs for those who adore children and want to work in areas related to their health. While many of these jobs focus on helping sick children, more and more jobs are related to the prevention of illness. Furthermore, new technologies permit doctors to treat conditions previously regarded as untreatable.

## What It's Like to Be a Pediatrician

Caring for children is as rewarding as ever for Dr. Gustave (Stavie) Kreh, who has been in pediatric practice for more than twenty-five years. This pediatrician adores children and was attracted to pediatrics after working in summer camps during high school and college. After graduation from high school, Stavie attended Tulane University in New Orleans, where he majored in sociology and minored in history and chemistry and took enough science courses to get into medical school.

After graduating from college, Stavie attended the Louisiana State School of Medicine in New Orleans. Medical school, according to Stavie, teaches the facts and skills that every pediatrician needs, but he believes that his liberal arts degree is what gave him the foundation to be an excellent doctor. He wants students who are contemplating becoming doctors to realize that medical school is a tough grind even for students who did well in high school and college. Most medical students are overwhelmed by the tremendous amount of study and memorization that is required in the first year. Stavie still remembers the first day of medical school when he could not even pronounce the words on the professors' mimeographed handouts. Challenged by the difficulty and amount of work that was required of him, he battled back by studying eight to ten hours a day at school and then four or five more hours in the library at night.

"By the end of the intense, four-year medical program," Stavie points out, "you are like a sculpture. You have been chiseled, beaten, sat on, molded, melted down, and refined into a finished product." However, the sculpture was not yet finished, as Stavie still had to complete a three-year residency in pediatrics. When he recalls those years, Stavie remembers they were "horrendous hours, lousy pay, and twenty-four-hour duty every third day." At the same time, they were enjoyable because he was doing what he wanted to be doing.

After completing an army tour, he joined a pediatric practice with four other doctors in Savannah, Georgia. Today, this practice has nine doctors in what is one of the largest pediatric practices in the Southeast, with more than fifty thousand patients. The office is open at 9 A.M., 365 days a year, and stays open until every child has been seen. However, on weekends and holidays only two doctors are in the office. Stavie designed the group's ten thousand-square-foot office building, which has separate waiting rooms with different themes for well babies, sick children, adolescents, and new babies. The group also has two satellite offices.

A typical weekday for Stavie starts at 6 A.M., when he checks with his answering service for messages from patients and reports from partners. Then it is off to the two hospitals that the group services, where it usually takes him anywhere from an hour to two hours to visit his patients and confer with the nurses on each patient's progress or any potential medical problems. Around 9 A.M., Stavie arrives at the office, where he sees an average of forty patients a day. On an extremely busy day, he could see up to eighty patients. While seeing so many patients may seem like assembly-line doctoring, Stavie says that most children have illnesses that are easily treated, such as headaches, colds, and infections of the ears, respiratory system, and skin. When the occasional emergency arises, however, the pediatricians drop everything and go to the hospital to take care of the child.

Prospective pediatricians need to remember that besides treating sick children, they also have to attend conferences, monthly pediatric meetings, staff meetings, and hospital committee meetings, as well as oversee finances, computer operations, telephone systems, laboratory equipment, and hiring and scheduling staff.

**Solid Advice.** To be a good pediatrician, Stavie feels it is necessary for you to like children, work fast, tolerate night calls from scared parents, have empathy with sick children, and have a sixth sense that helps you determine what is wrong when children cannot really explain their ailments.

**The Rewards.** The happiest moments on the job for Stavie come when he is able to save a child from a life-threatening illness. He also loves having children drop by to see him before they go off to college just to talk. Stavie's patients are like family to him, and he finds it very rewarding to see them grow both physically and emotionally.

## What It's Like to Be a Pediatric Specialist

Pediatricians and family practitioners are the primary medical caregivers for children. However, they are aided in their work by specialists in the many health care fields mentioned earlier. Tom Southern, a plastic surgeon, is one of those specialists. During his junior year of medical school, he became totally hooked on a career as a plastic surgeon after seeing the difference a plastic surgeon could make in the life of a burned child. Today, 25 percent of his practice is devoted to the care of children.

A look at Tom's work schedule shows that he is very busy. The most difficult part of his job is trying to accomplish everything that he wants to get done. Every Monday and Wednesday, Tom is sees patients in his office from 9 A.M. to 5 P.M. However, his day neither begins at 9 A.M. nor ends at 5 P.M. Before office hours, Tom visits patients in two hospitals, and after office hours he continues seeing hospital patients until 7 P.M. On Tuesday, Thursday, and Friday, Tom is usually in surgery by 8 A.M., continuing until 3 P.M. or sometimes 6 P.M. Three times a month he is on call in the hospital emergency room, and he also has to take his turn on call in his own private practice. Tom spends his days treating traumas and burns and doing reconstructive surgery. He has treated children who are as young as one month old.

What Tom likes most about plastic surgery is the variety of surgical procedures that he performs and the different personalities of his patients. However, he dislikes his lack of free time. His advice to anyone who is planning to enter the medical profession, and especially plastic surgery, is to be prepared to immerse yourself in your job but find time for yourself and your family.

## What It's Like to Be a Pediatric Nurse

Pediatric nurses are registered nurses specially trained to provide nursing services to infants, children, and adolescents. They usually work in doctors' offices, hospitals, and clinics. Dan Smith entered this profession because he loved working with children. A typical day at work for him involves seeing about twenty-five patients for well-baby appointments, physicals, and treating sick children. Between appointments, Dan returns phone calls to answer questions from anxious parents about their children's health. According to Dan, pediatric nurses need physical examination and assessment skills plus the ability to discuss the medical needs of children in terms the parents can understand. What he likes most about his job is dealing with children. The least favorite part of his job is dealing with difficult parents.

### Earnings

Pediatricians are generally well paid, earning an average salary of more than $152,000 a year. Those in pediatric specialties can expect higher incomes. The average salary for full-time registered nurses is now more than $48,000 a year. Some earn more than $70,000 a year. Licensed practical nurses earn more than $31,000 a year, with some nurses earning more than $44,000 a year. In addition to common benefits—paid vacation, sick leave, and medical and life insurance—many nurses receive child care, education benefits, and bonuses from their employers.

# Taking Care of Children's Teeth

The cute smiles of children with gaps between their front teeth are very appealing to everyone. Little children need dental care to avoid having dental problems as adults. The way gums and baby teeth are cared for affects the development of adult teeth. To ensure that their smiles remain perfect, young children go to pediatric dentists, pediatric hygienists, orthodontists, and general practitioners of dentistry.

Although the demand for dentists is not expected to grow as fast as the average of all occupations through the year 2012, the demand for dental hygienists and dental assistants is expected to grow much faster as they take on more of the routine services now performed by dentists.

## Earnings

Most dentists are self-employed businesspeople with offices and a support staff of assistants, receptionists, and hygienists. According to the American Dental Association, after expenses, a dentist in private practice earns more than $173,000 a year. Salaried dentists earn approximately $123,000 a year. Dentists often earn less, however, in the beginning years of their practices. The average earnings of dental assistants is more than $13 an hour, with some earning close to $20 per hour. Hygienists, like assistants, are paid an hourly wage that varies by location, employment setting, and experience. Experienced dental hygienists average more than $26 per hour, with some earning close to $40 an hour.

## What It's Like to Be a Children's Dentist

In dental school, Donald Bozic found that he was attracted to pediatric dentistry, as he was able to communicate well with children and enjoyed treating them. As soon as he graduated from dental school and was licensed to practice dentistry, he began his practice in pediatric dentistry. Donald needed substantial training to become a pediatric dentist, which included:

- four years of college (B.S. in chemistry)
- four years of dental school
- two years of specialty training (residency in a hospital for children)

Without his specialty training, Donald could not have limited his practice to children's dentistry. A typical day for him begins at about 8 A.M. and finishes at approximately 5 P.M. He takes about one hour for lunch. His clients include a mixture of very young children, school-age children, and even college students.

According to Donald, these are the special skills that you need to be a good pediatric dentist:

- extraordinary patience
- ability to listen
- excellent dental skills
- ability to work quickly
- ability to work well with children

His work environment is definitely child friendly. It is an open, airy office with a special monkey room where hundreds of stuffed toy monkeys cling to the wall. Each young patient can select one of the monkeys to hold while his or her teeth are treated. Donald's happiest moments on the job come when he is able to give children a positive attitude toward dentistry.

## What It's Like to Be a Children's Dental Hygienist

Marcia Bozic is an active member of her husband's dental team as a registered dental hygienist. Three years of specialized training are required to become a dental hygienist. Marcia sees young patients who are scheduled for thirty- to forty-five-minute appointments for cleaning, x-rays, fluoride treatment, and dental education. She prefers working with children because it is so much fun to talk with them. And when children walk out of the office, they do so happily because of her skills and personality. Yes, there are children who like to visit the dentist when the hygienist is Marcia. With great big smiles, they walk out wearing rings, carrying stickers and a new toothbrush, and holding their dental report cards.

# Counseling Troubled Children

Not all children are happy and well-adjusted. Some children are depressed, don't know how to make friends, have low self-esteem, have been sexually abused, or need to know how to cope with problems such as learning disabilities or their parents' divorce. Stepping in to help these children are psychiatrists, psychologists, and counselors. All of these health care professionals are highly trained individuals with years of postgraduate education. They all share a common bond of wanting to give troubled children the tools and skills to handle their problems so that they have the best chance at a healthy adulthood.

## Child Psychiatrists

When children have problems, most of them first turn to their friends, parents, and teachers for help. Child psychiatrists deal primarily with children who need more than advice and a chance to talk things over. Only psychiatrists can prescribe drugs in the treatment of psychological problems. They often use medication in the treatment of such disorders as ADD (attention deficit disorder), schizophrenia, Tourette's syndrome, depression, sleeping difficulties, and bed-wetting problems. Child psychiatrists typically work in private offices, clinics, and hospitals. Psychiatrists must be medical doctors before taking at least three more years of training in psychiatry.

## Child Psychologists

More than one-third of all psychologists work primarily in elementary and secondary schools, where they counsel and test children. A master's degree in psychology is sufficient for working in schools. However, psychologists in private practice or those who offer any type of patient care in clinical, counseling, and school psychology must meet certification or licensing requirements. Most psychologists in clinical settings or private practice have doctoral degrees, which they receive after three to five years of graduate work. Their work hours usually reflect the hours when children are available, so many work evenings and weekends.

## What It's Like to Be a Child Psychologist

It's not easy to become a child psychologist. After graduating from college with a double major in psychology and fine arts, Susan Schwartz spent eight years in graduate school, an internship, and a postdoctoral fellowship before she could even take her state's test to become a licensed psychologist. Susan chose this career, with its long and arduous preparation, because she wanted to have an impact on children's lives at a time when they needed help. Right from the start of her graduate training, she was able to work with children. While she was always supervised in her dealings with children, the level of supervision lessened as she continued in the program. In becoming a child psychologist, Susan had a wide range of clinical experiences. She tested schoolchildren for learning disabilities, counseled children with behavioral problems, and evaluated children with severe psychiatric difficulties, such as experiencing hallucinations and suicidal or homicidal thoughts, for hospital admission. Her workplaces included schools, hospital emergency rooms, and in-service clinics. The final step for Susan was passing the licensing examination given by her state, which allowed her to supervise other psychologists, sign off on psychological evaluations, and get third-party payments from insurance companies.

## What It's Like to Be a Children's Counselor

Counselors cannot do therapy with children unless they are licensed by the state in which they practice. Mary Gail Nelson holds an MFCC (marriage, family, and child counselor) license in the state of California. To get this license she had to earn a master's in counseling or a related area plus complete three thousand hours of internship. Half of those hours had to be earned after she received her master's degree. According to Mary Gail, the process, from starting a master's degree to getting a license, takes from five to six years. She also holds a lifetime teaching credential, which is helpful in her practice with schoolchildren.

The focus of Mary Gail's practice is families and children. She may see the children alone or with their families. On a typical day, Mary Gail may help the children of divorcing parents work out their feelings through art, games, role playing, and talking. She may also see a child who is hitting others, where her objective is to help the child explore options other than hitting when he or she is angry at another child at school. Besides counseling children and their families, Mary Gail holds workshops at schools to help parents learn what children really need from them. She also may be called to testify in a child custody suit.

## Earnings

Psychiatrists typically earn considerably more than either psychologists or counselors. A psychiatrist can expect to earn more than $163,000 a year. Psychologists with doctoral degrees average approximately $73,000 a year, while those with master's degrees earn around $34,000. School psychologists average more than $54,000, while school counselors earn the same as teachers with equivalent degrees and experience, about $45,000. Marriage and family counselors earn about $35,000.

# Speech-Language Pathologists

Another career that lets people who adore children really improve children's lives is speech-language pathology. In this profession, you work with children who stutter, lisp, cannot pronounce some sounds correctly, or have some other problem with their speech. Through treatment and therapy, you help children improve their speech. Your work setting could be a hospital, clinic, private practice, or group practice, but you are more likely to be employed at a school. At a school, you may work with just one child or a small group of children. You occasionally help teachers in the classroom with activities that meet the special needs of children with speech disorders. Part of your job in any setting is counseling parents and telling them how they can help their children. Quite often you give children homework assignments in which they work on certain sounds, and parents are able to help their children complete this work.

To work as a speech-language pathologist, most states require you have a master's degree. Not all states require you to be licensed, but those that do have demanding requirements. You need a master's degree or equivalent; 300 to 375 hours of supervised clinical experience; a passing score on a national examination; and nine months of postgraduate professional clinical experience. To get your license renewed, you may have to fulfill continuing education requirements. If you wish to earn a Certificate of Clinical Competence in speech-language pathology, you need to earn a graduate degree, complete 375 hours of supervised clinical experience and a thirty-six-week postgraduate clinical fellowship, and pass a written examination.

## Demand for Speech-Language Pathologists

The employment picture is excellent for speech-language pathologists who want to work with children due to a greater awareness of the importance of early identification, diagnosis, and treatment of speech and language disorders. More people in this profession are now being employed by schools as federal law guarantees special education and related services to all eligible children with disabilities.

The average salary for full-time speech-language pathologists with one to three years of experience is approximately $42,000. The average salary for all certified speech-language pathologists is $48,000, according to the American Speech-Language Hearing Association. Those who work in schools average $46,000.

## Rewards for Health Care Professionals

Choose a career as a health care professional and society will hold you in high esteem for your services as a lifesaver and a health care provider. By wielding your skills, you will be able to help children recover from illnesses and accidents as well as stay healthy. Your career will be fantastically satisfying because you will be helping the children you adore.

# CHAPTER NINE

# Child Welfare Careers

*Definition: Child welfare workers improve
the lives of disadvantaged children.*

Today's children are tomorrow's teachers, politicians, computer experts, factory workers, and financial gurus. In a perfect world, all children would have a safe, happy childhood. This is sometimes difficult to provide in a world that is not always kind to children. Pick up a newspaper and all too often you'll see a headline describing children who are abused or neglected by their families. Magazines contain articles about elementary school-children carrying guns and selling drugs. Radio and television programs report on elementary and middle school gang activity. We hear and read about newborns suffering through withdrawal symptoms because their mothers used drugs. The media focuses great attention on all the problems children face in their homes, schools, and lives. Unfortunately, an incredible number of children desperately need help. Much of this help is provided by compassionate, hard-working individuals who have careers in the areas of child welfare and juvenile justice.

If you wish to work with children, consider a career in one of these areas, where you can truly improve children's lives. Job opportunities include working as a social worker, police officer, juvenile court judge, probation officer, juvenile court referee, and child advocate. No matter what you choose to do, you will be a steadfast support to children who really need your help.

# Social Workers

The jobs in social work that deal directly with helping children are in the fields of child welfare and family services, children's protective services, and school services. Typically, social workers specialize in one field. Let's look at what a social worker's job would involve in each field:

- **Child welfare and family services social workers** often act as counselors, helping young people who are having serious problems. They may also find foster homes or arrange adoptions for neglected, abandoned, or abused children.
- **Children's protective services social workers** probably have the most stressful jobs among all social workers. They are responsible for investigating reports of child abuse and neglect. They may have to remove children from their homes and place them in emergency shelters or with foster families. The social workers continue to monitor these children until they are returned to their families or are permanently placed in another environment.
- **School services social workers** handle children's problems at school, such as misbehavior in class and too many absences. They advise teachers on how to deal with problem students. Also, school services social workers may be involved in helping disabled children adjust to school.

## The Employment Picture

If you decide that you would like to be a social worker, you would probably work for a state or local government. You are also likely to be employed in a city or suburb rather than a rural area. Although you are only supposed to work a forty-hour week, your hours will not necessarily be confined to nine to five. Emergencies sometimes occur outside those hours. Furthermore, you may have to meet with children and their parents or foster parents in the evenings or on weekends. As you climb the career ladder, your work tends to become more supervisory and to involve less direct contact with children.

While social work is a satisfying career, it can be emotionally draining. Plus, understaffing and large caseloads add to the pressure in some agencies.

## Demand for Social Workers

Growing concern about juvenile crime and children and families in crisis situations has increased the demand for social workers in both government and private agencies. There are now approximately half a million social workers. In the future, the number of social workers in the private sector is anticipated to increase as the government increasingly contracts out social services. This occupation will grow faster than the average for all occupations through 2012. The number of school social workers is especially expected to increase due to rising enrollment and continued emphasis on integrating disabled children into the general school population.

## Earnings

Social work does not pay well for the amount of education required even to get a job. The average income of child, family, and school social workers is more than $33,000 a year. While the bottom 10 percent of workers earn less than $22,000, the highest 10 percent earn more than $54,000. You should know that social workers' salaries vary depending on where they live and where they work. The county caseworkers and supervisors who make the most money usually live in the central part of the United States, and city caseworkers tend to make more money than those employed by states and counties.

## Education and Certification

Social workers must have a bachelor's degree in social work, psychology, sociology, or a related field to get even an entry-level job. And for many jobs as well as career advancement, a master's degree, preferably in social work (M.S.W.), is becoming essential. With an M.S.W. degree, social workers are qualified to manage cases, supervise other workers, and handle clinical work. Master's programs typically take two years to complete and include a minimum of nine hundred hours of supervised field instruction or internship. The Council on Social Work Education (CSWE) publishes the *Directory of Colleges and Universities with Accredited Social Work Degree Programs*, or you can find schools on the organization's website. For more information, contact CSWE at:

Council on Social Work Education
1725 Duke Street, Suite 500
Alexandria, VA 22314
www.cswe.org

Besides having the requisite degrees, social workers in every state must be licensed, certified, or registered in order to work. Voluntary certification is offered by the National Association of Social Workers to those who qualify. Such credentials are very important for those who are in private practice as some health insurers will only reimburse certified social workers.

## What It's Like to Be a Social Worker in Children's Protective Services

Armed with a bachelor's degree in social work, Nick Costa started looking for a job as a social worker only to discover that many departments of social services in his state would not hire inexperienced social workers unless they held a master's degree. Through a counselor in his college social work internship program, Nick heard about a job at a mental health contract agency, where he worked for two years helping to mainstream mental health clients out of hospitals and board and care facilities. Because this first job did not pay well, Nick continued to search for a better job. A job hotline call to another county brought a job in children's protective services to Nick's attention. He prepared seriously for his job interview by talking to actual workers in the field to learn exactly what they did on the job.

Nick was hired along with three others to work in children's protective services in a small, overworked department. He was assigned to the family reunification program, where he received on-the-job training from his supervisor and coworkers. He learned how to investigate reports of child abuse, how to write reports for the juvenile court, and how to monitor children's placements in foster homes. The main task of reunification workers is to help parents regain custody of children who have been placed in foster homes by the juvenile court. The parents are provided a total of twelve to eighteen months to meet the conditions set for reunification. If reunification is not possible, a permanent plan of adoption, guardianship, or placement with a relative is sought. Only when none of these is possible does long-term foster care become the permanent plan for the child.

After six months, the family reunification program was combined with the family maintenance program and the permanent placement program. This approach is called generic or seamless case management and results in fewer transfers of children from caseworker to caseworker. Besides trying to reunite families, Nick was trying to keep families together in the family maintenance program and making permanent plans for children who could not be returned to their parents. Coworkers showed him how to handle his new responsibilities, which included vast amounts of paperwork. Nick next worked for eighteen months in a special placement unit, where he was responsible for the placement of children in group homes or treatment facilities because of their behavioral or psychiatric problems. Then he returned to his prior job as a generic social worker, and, with five years of experience, found he had reached the top of the pay scale for social workers at his agency. Nick decided to change jobs because there was no foreseeable possibility of advancement to a supervisory position.

Nick's next job was in a suburban area, where he received considerably more pay. At first, his job was the same as his earlier one.

Then he moved to emergency response work in which he had to decide within a few hours or even minutes whether children were in such risk of abuse that they had to be removed from their families. He did emergency response work for almost six months. In his next move within this agency, Nick became the lead worker in a unit to train new social workers. After this unit was disbanded because of budget cuts, he returned to a family reunification unit. Because Nick did not have a master's degree, he was not able to continue to climb the career ladder at this job, so he moved to another agency where a master's degree was not a requirement to become a supervisor.

Although the procedures for being a social worker in children's protective services vary depending on where you work, Nick finds that working with children is the one main positive in his job that never changes. Because of their backgrounds, most of these children have not received appropriate attention. They are usually eager for attention from a parental figure. Nick has taken a child out for ice cream and later learned that the child still talked about it a year later. Nick gives every child he works with his card. And he finds that they sometimes hang on to it for long periods of time because it represents security and a lifeline to them. Nick says children want to be able to trust adults and can tell when you are really trying to help them. This makes the social worker a very important person to them and gives you an opportunity to have a positive impact on their lives. It is also a very big responsibility.

# Police in Youth Services Departments

Police officers in small communities and rural areas have a wide variety of duties that often include working with children. In large communities, the police officers who work with young people are usually specifically assigned to the youth services department. Within this department, officers work with runaway juveniles, gang members, abused children, and children who are suspected of breaking the law. They also work as liaison officers with schools, where officers teach the children about personal and traffic safety and substance abuse. Most officers find considerable satisfaction in their work with children because they can see the children's lives improving because of their efforts.

## Job Outlook and Earnings

Because of the increase in juvenile crime and child abuse, as well as more police officers being assigned to school liaison work, the outlook is good for jobs in youth services departments. Overall, the employment of police officers is expected to increase faster than the average for all occupations through 2012, although how many officers are actually hired will depend on budgetary constraints. Nevertheless, because many officers are able to retire in their forties, there is always a need for replacements.

Police officers in nonsupervisory positions earn average annual salaries of more than $42,000. The lowest 10 percent earn less than $26,000 a year; the highest 10 percent earn more than $65,000. Officers who hold supervisory positions average more than $61,000 anually. Total earnings often exceed salaries because of payments for overtime work. Also, earnings do vary by geographic location, with salaries generally being higher in large cities and western states.

## Qualifications for Police Officers

Your character and background are very important factors when you apply for a job as a police officer. You must be able to show that you are honest and responsible and possess good judgment. In large police departments, candidates usually must be high school graduates.

However, a growing number of cities and states are requiring some postsecondary education. Also, police departments are now hiring college graduates with degrees in law enforcement or administration of justice. In order to become eligible for an appointment, you must perform well on written examinations and pass a physical examination.

## What It's Like to Be "Officer Friendly"

At sixteen, David Nye joined a police explorer scout program that convinced him that being a police officer was his life's work. After high school, David was hired as a police cadet and worked twenty hours a week while he was enrolled full-time in college. When he was twenty-one and a junior in college, David became a police officer after passing all the tests and attending the police academy. In the suburban police department where David is now employed, college work is encouraged, and the city pays for college tuition. David holds an associate's degree in administration of justice, a bachelor's degree in public safety, a master's in public administration and organization, and is considering obtaining a doctorate.

David started his police work in patrol services and worked for a while as a detective after appropriate in-service training. He then returned to patrol services and later joined the juvenile bureau. David has been with the juvenile bureau since 1985.

At first, David spent most of his time in the juvenile bureau on such cases as runaways and suspects of criminal action. However, 20 percent of his time was spent being Officer Friendly. Many police departments across the country have Officer Friendly programs. As Officer Friendly, David went to schools, from preschool through high school, and talked to children in their classrooms. David talked to the youngest children about personal and traffic safety and even ran bicycle safety rodeos for them. He addressed the older children on the consequences and effects of drugs and gangs. And he talked to the high school students about driver's education, drugs, drinking, and civics and law issues.

After one year, David began to work full-time in the schools as Officer Friendly and decided he wanted to expand the program. He integrated the program with D.A.R.E. (Drug Abuse Resistance Education) in order to place more emphasis on antidrug work. All of the area schools wanted this program, and it grew steadily until three officers were working full-time and a fourth officer worked part-time.

Today, David works in schools from 8 A.M. to 3 P.M., Tuesday through Thursday. After school, he talks about drug abuse and other problems with children, their parents, and school staff. He also does after-school programs with youth sports and other positive alternatives to drugs and gangs. David rotates through the grades in each school, spending more time in fifth and eighth grades, where he visits each class for forty-five minutes a week for a semester to concentrate on the D.A.R.E. message against drug use. He is still Officer Friendly in his visits to the younger children. David loves his work and believes that he is helping children make responsible decisions by emphasizing how they can take care of themselves and avoid substance abuse, gangs, and other high-risk behaviors.

# Jobs Within the Juvenile Justice System

The juvenile justice system is not a large career field, but it does offer careers as a juvenile judge, court referee, probation officer, caseworker, or lawyer. Opportunities for volunteer service exist for court-appointed special advocates for children. Each state sets up its own system, so job titles and responsibilities vary state by state. You are more likely to have a job dealing only with children if you work in a large city or a heavily populated area. Nevertheless, no matter what career you pursue within juvenile justice, it is a perfect job for those who truly want to help troubled children.

## Juvenile Court Judges

To pursue a career as a juvenile court judge, you must first become a lawyer and practice law. To become a juvenile court judge, you usually must run for office, be elected, be chosen to fill out the term of an incumbent, or be appointed. Only in large cities are judges able to concentrate solely on juvenile justice. In rural areas, judges hear all kinds of cases and may only devote one day a month to juvenile justice cases.

As a juvenile court judge, you would hear cases involving children who commit crimes from shoplifting to major felonies. You also hear cases involving crimes such as truancy, smoking, and running away, charges that would not be crimes if committed by adults. Your goal is always rehabilitation, and you work closely with probation officers, social workers, caseworkers, and the police to see that this goal is achieved. Besides hearing cases in which children commit crimes, you hear cases in which crimes are committed against children. Then it is your task, with the help of social workers and others in the community, to see that the children are protected.

To be a judge, you need a wide range of skills. Of course, judges must be honest and fair minded. They also must possess good oral and written communication skills. Judges need to be good organizers and able to direct the work of others. Juvenile court judges have the professional responsibility of studying continually. They must know about such things as the impact of dysfunctional families on children and the success of specific substance abuse programs.

Judges must be willing to work long hours. Even though juvenile court judges are not the best-paid judges, many devote their careers to this area because of their dedication to and concern for children.

## Juvenile Court Referees

Courts throughout the country are continually short of money, and yet more and more demands are being made on juvenile court judges. To assist judges, juvenile court referees, also called masters, act as judges, resolving cases involving children. If the parties involved in the case do not like the decision of the referee, they can appeal to the judge for review. Referees are among the busiest people in the judicial system. At times, they may handle as many as one hundred cases a day. Referees usually hold bachelor's degrees in the social sciences and have related juvenile or casework experience. Ninety-five percent of referees are trained in law.

## Child Advocates—a Child's Friend in Court

Every year almost three hundred thousand children are removed from their homes because they live with chemically dependent parents or they are victims of sexual abuse, physical abuse, or abandonment by their parents. It is up to a judge to decide if the children will be reunited with their parents, placed in foster care, or adopted. Overworked judges, caseworkers, social workers, and lawyers simply don't have the time to thoroughly study each case. This is where a child advocate steps in. Judges appoint child advocates who make recommendations to them on placement options for children. First and foremost, child advocates speak for the children. They want what is best for them. To figure this out, child advocates talk to the children, parents, social workers, foster parents, teachers, doctors, neighbors, and therapists.

Child advocates are not paid. They are volunteers trained in courtroom procedure, social service, and the special needs of children who have been abused and neglected. For those who adore children, being a child advocate is an opportunity to help a child find a safe, permanent home and at the same time learn more about the juvenile justice system.

# Helping Children with Serious Problems

With countless children involved in substance abuse and crimes and so many children being taken from their parents in order to protect them, an enormous number of troubled children need the support of professionals who have careers in child welfare and juvenile justice. In this chapter, we explored how social workers, police officers, juvenile court judges, referees, and child advocates play a role in assisting these children. Of course, there are many other jobs within child welfare and juvenile justice that are designed to help children, such as probation officers, lawyers, and counselors. Career satisfaction is very high for those who safeguard the welfare of children because they are giving seriously troubled children a chance at a better future.

# CHAPTER TEN

# Arts and Entertainment Careers

*Definition: Arts and entertainment workers share
their knowledge of the arts with children and offer
a wide variety of opportunities to be entertained.*

Beyond their daily routines, children need the extra dimension in their lives that can come from entertainment and the arts. They should experience the special gifts of art, music, dance, and the theater. They need to feel the magic of the moment as a performance unfolds before their eyes and the satisfaction that comes from painting a picture, playing an instrument, or dancing. There's also the wonderful joy that comes from being entertained by clowns, magicians, and other performers. When kids at heart choose careers in this fascinating field, they can be part of the dividends that arts and entertainment bring to young children. For those who both love arts and entertainment and adore children, careers exist that can satisfy these two enthusiasms.

## Careers in the Arts

Children learn about art, music, dance, and theater in school. Some children, however, want to extend their knowledge of the arts through lessons that let them explore a particular art in depth. Many career options are available for those who wish to share their skills in the arts. For example, you could teach music to the neighborhood children or a prodigy at Juilliard. While most arts careers for kids at heart focus on teaching the arts to children, it is possible to find other careers such as painting portraits of children and creating music for them.

# A Career as an Art Teacher

You do not have to paint like Rembrandt, Michelangelo, or Monet to find work teaching young people how to draw, paint, or sculpt. While only a limited number of your students will ever become professional artists, you will be able to help most of them gain an appreciation of art through your classes. Artists who desire to share their love of art with children will find teaching them a rewarding career. Individuals wishing to teach art in public schools need a bachelor's degree in education with training in art education. Also, most teachers obtain their master's degrees early in their teaching careers.

Artists who want to work with children are not confined to working in public schools. They can also teach art in art museums and for art associations and in their own homes.

## What It's Like to Teach Art from the Cart

Sonia Fernandez is an elementary school art teacher. She has taught in beautiful, fully equipped art rooms, in cafeterias, and in science rooms; she has also pushed a cart loaded with art supplies from room to room. In an elementary school, teaching art can be a hectic experience. Art teachers never seem to have enough time to get everything done. Supplies have to be taken out and put back for each class, and a project must be completed in thirty or forty-five minutes. According to Sonia, an hour would be an ideal amount of time for an art class, especially for students in the intermediate grades, but this rarely happens. Art teachers in public schools need to realize that they may see every student in a school during the course of a week. This often means teaching art to more than five hundred students.

Art teachers also have demands made on their time to prepare such things as posters for paper drives and props or scenery for school musicals or plays, and they help children participate in art competitions. Add in the frustration of crowded classrooms, and you might wonder why Sonia enjoys teaching art and would not think of teaching any other class. The reason is simple: she thoroughly enjoys introducing children to the world of art.

## A Career as a Child Portraitist

As an artist who portrays children for a living, you would be a member of a very small career field. Nevertheless, a few artists become famous for their representations of children. Mary Cassatt was one of these artists. She remains one of America's most famous woman painters, known for her pictures of mothers and children. While you may never achieve the fame of Mary Cassatt, you may be able to have an art career specializing in the painting or sculpting of children. Only the most successful artists are able to support themselves solely through the sale of their works. Many also work in galleries or in some administrative capacity related to the arts or teach art to support themselves.

## A Career as a Music Teacher

Teaching music is an excellent way to share a love of music with children—from fledgling musicians in preschool to skilled older children. Each age level offers different challenges and rewards, and prospective music teachers may want to focus on a particular age group. You can teach music to children in elementary schools. You can teach in your home, their homes, music stores, or studios. Learn more about careers in teaching music by contacting:

National Association for Music Education
1806 Robert Fulton Drive
Reston, VA 20191
www.manc.org

The association publishes two helpful brochures: "Careers in Music" and "Why Teach, Why Music, Why Me?"

To learn even more about teaching music to children, you can study professional journals, such as these publications found in university libraries and some public libraries:

*The American Music Teacher*
*The American String Teacher*
*Music Educators' Journal*
*The Choral Journal*

## Private Music Instructors

Being a private music teacher is an excellent way for a musician to work closely with children. How many students a teacher will have depends on the demand in the area as well as the individual's reputation as a skilled teacher. Since most of their students are in school during the day, a private teacher's workday does not normally begin until the end of the school day. Fees usually range from $25 to $60 per lesson, although some experts command fees as high as $150 per lesson.

## What It's Like to Be a Music Teacher

Melissa Williams has taught music in elementary school and worked at a residential treatment center for emotionally disturbed children. Today, she teaches tuba, euphonium, and trombone to about forty students, plays in symphony orchestras in two cities, and does some freelancing at recording studios making music tapes. To get started as a private teacher in a new city, Melissa joined a brass choir and played with a local symphony, where she met many school music teachers who recommended her to students in their classes. In her free time, Melissa practices the tuba, hoping to win an audition to be a regular in a major symphony orchestra. To hone her skills, this accomplished musician takes lessons from an expert player with the Chicago Symphony. Her educational background in music is solid, as she has a bachelor's degree in music with a minor in music therapy and a master's in music performance.

# A Career as a Dance Teacher

Children just naturally dance; they can hardly keep their bodies still. Furthermore, they enjoy perfecting their skills through dance classes. Millions of dollars are spent every year for dance lessons, from preschoolers learning to tap and do ballet to junior high school students learning social dancing. Teachers are needed to train all these eager dancers in a variety of settings, such as day-care centers, public schools, dance schools, conservatories, studios, and special education programs.

Teaching dance gives you an opportunity to actually dance with children as you do your job. Do you think that you possess the special skills and knowledge needed to teach dance to children? Ask yourself the following questions:

1. Do you have an anatomical understanding of how the body works?
2. Do you have the ability to relate to children of different ages?
3. Do you enjoy music?
4. Do you have the ability to choreograph dances for children?
5. Do you have the patience to teach the same step over and over?
6. Do you have the organizational skills needed to break a dance down into parts and then reteach each part until the whole dance has been mastered?

7. Do you have the skills necessary to keep discipline in a class?
8. Do you possess a sense of rhythm?
9. Are you able to express ideas, moods, and emotions through dance movements?
10. Are you self-confident?
11. Are you creative?
12. Are you able to work under pressure?
13. Do you have ambition?
14. Do you have talent?
15. Are you willing to spend long hours in training and practice?
16. Do you have good physical endurance?
17. Do you have leadership ability?
18. Do you have a love of dancing and a sincere interest in teaching dance to children?

Future children's dance teachers will answer yes to almost every one of the above questions. To actually teach dance, the training and educational background needed depend on the type of dance you wish to teach and where you want to teach. Many private dance teachers have trained since early childhood, and their own personal background acts as the foundation of their teaching. Most of these dancers continue their own lessons and practice sessions even after they have started to teach dance. If you want to teach dance in a public school, however, you need to earn the necessary academic degrees and credentials just like other teachers in the educational system.

## What It's Like to Teach Dancing and Etiquette

Rebecca Kreuger Malenkos majored in English in college and became an English teacher, but her true love has always been dancing. She started taking dance lessons at the age of four and studied ballet, tap, jazz, and ballroom dancing for more than thirteen years. In high school, she not only danced but was also in the choir and in musical productions. By the time Rebecca was in tenth grade, she had become a student assistant at the ballroom dancing school for young people where she had taken lessons in social dancing and etiquette since she was in sixth grade. She gained even more teaching experience in college through teaching ballroom dancing. After college, Rebecca operated her own school in Texas called Rebecca's Cotillion, where she taught dance etiquette and such basic ballroom dances as the fox trot, waltz, swing, and tango. After moving to Indianapolis, she reopened Rebecca's Cotillion. Operating her school involves more than just teaching dance. Students have to receive written invitations, publicity must be done to advertise the school, and Rebecca has to solve the logistical problem of having an equal number of boys and girls for each class.

## Organizations for Dance Teachers

If you want to teach dance to children, you can acquire solid information from dance associations. Prospective dance teachers should also read the publications of these associations to keep abreast of what is happening in dance. And they should consider attending association conventions to meet dance teachers and watch demonstrations of the latest dance techniques. In the Appendix, you will find the names and addresses of professional organizations that have helpful information for prospective dance teachers.

# Careers in Entertainment

Behind the scenes or in front of an audience, there are careers for kids at heart who want to entertain children. Circus performers have always experienced the joy of entertaining children; however, opportunities now exist in radio, television, movies, and the theater. Many enterprising individuals have started their own businesses by focusing on entertaining children at parties and schools.

Often jobs related to children are only part-time. However, there is full-time employment in shows at year-round amusement parks and at television stations devoted to programs only for children.

## What It's Like to Be a Magician

Steve Hart shows children a book about fishing, and a fish squirts water on him. When they see a book about banking, money pops out. The book on Aladdin breathes smoke. Steve is a magician who does reading motivational programs in schools as well as working at marketing trade and sales shows for adults. His "Magic of Reading" show for children combines entertainment with the theme of reading. It is a fast-paced, thought-provoking program that encourages children to read and emphasizes the importance of the alphabet, words, and reading. And, of course, it begins with the magical books that he takes from his reading treasure chest. With a little more magic carefully applied to them during his performance, all the books in the chest turn to gold, and Steve has sparked the children's interest in reading.

The day President Kennedy died, a magician came to Steve's school and made the children forget what had happened for a little while. Then and there, Steve, who was only in fifth grade, knew that he would become a magician. He went to the library and checked out books on magic and received a magician's kit as a gift from his parents. According to Steve, the only schooling that is really helpful in becoming a magician is teaching yourself. You study and practice, practice, practice until you gain skill. Of course, it is essential to have excellent eye-hand coordination, and a background in theater can make your performance more dramatic. Steve points out that you can never stand still as a magician; you must always be improving and looking for new and exciting ways to entertain. Steve has invented several tricks, including one where he makes a two-liter bottle of pop disappear right before your eyes. He fills his shows with wonderful, colorful displays and even live doves and rabbits.

Steve immersed himself completely in magic once he made the decision to become a magician. By the time he was in eighth grade, he was such a good magician that he replaced the magician who had inspired his career and performed a magic show for the whole school. He went on to win first place in a national magician contest in which magicians from around the country participated.

Being a magician is a very small career field. There are only about a thousand full-time magicians in the country. Most magicians are amateurs. Starting as a young magician, you can earn from $25 to $50 for a performance. Full-time magicians like Steve can earn from $20,000 to $100,000 per year, and superstar magicians earn even more.

Steve strongly advises anyone interested in magic to become a member of the International Brotherhood of Magicians (IBM). Members, who can be as young as ten, receive a monthly magazine, *Linking Ring*, devoted to the history of magic and the techniques involved in performing tricks. There is even a special section for young magicians. Local chapters of IBM, called rings, have monthly meetings, and there are also international conventions. Steve believes that it is very important for magicians to belong to a fellowship organization and be able to mix with other magicians. At present, there are nearly fifteen thousand IBM members worldwide.

Steve's happiest moments as a magician occur whenever he appears before a group of children who have never seen a magician before and dazzles them with his magic. The only downside to being a magician is all the sales and marketing he is required to do to secure engagements.

## What It's Like to Be a Clown

Randy Blades is Krackles T. Clown. In case you are wondering, the *T* stands for *the*. Randy's career was launched when he went with Steve Hart to a magic convention and had his face painted as a clown. When he looked in a mirror, he fell in love with being a clown. That day, Krackles T. Clown was born. As Krackles, Randy started making balloon animals for children and then worked a series of shows. In his first year as a clown, he only made $10,000. However, he persevered, and today he is scarcely able to keep up with all the programs he is requested to do at child care centers, birthday parties, conventions, and on television. Plus, he works several restaurants each week on their family nights. For several years, he and Steve had their own television show, "Wacky Morning Cartoon Club," which will be back on the air again soon to delight children.

Randy is usually in clown makeup four times a week. When he first started making up his face, it took him over an hour, but now it only takes fifteen minutes. On a typical workday, Randy may do performances at 9 A.M. and 10:15 A.M. at child care centers. Then he may be off to a birthday party at 1 P.M., followed by two more child care centers in the afternoon. In the evening, he may perform at a corporate event.

Randy feels that he was born to be a clown. All he needs is makeup, magic, and balloons to be a successful entertainer. What he enjoys most about his job is making children and adults laugh, especially bringing out the child hidden in every adult. Like Steve, the only thing he dislikes about being a clown is having to generate business.

## A Career in Children's Television

Who can forget watching all the characters on Sesame Street or Mr. Rogers visiting with Lady Elaine? Besides the many public and network shows for children, many local stations also broadcast shows featuring homegrown television stars interacting on camera with children—a perfect job for the kid at heart who also wants to be in the limelight. This is a very small career field, and the competition for jobs is intense, for there are far more job-seekers than jobs. Formal training in communications from a college or technical school can be helpful in getting a first job in this field, as can being an intern at a television station.

# A Career in Children's Theater

Throughout the country, there are theatrical groups that focus on presenting the finest professional theater for young people. A few groups offer year-round employment to a professional staff. One of these groups is the Children's Theatre Company of Minneapolis. Each year the company presents six exceptional productions drawn from classic tales and challenging, original material created by the company. Besides presenting theatrical productions, the company offers a variety of educational programs, including a year-long acting apprentice program for adults ages eighteen to twenty-eight and instruction in movement, acting, and voice classes for preschoolers to teenagers. The educational program increases the number of job opportunities for kids at heart who are interested in the theater.

The Children's Theatre Company's full-time staff includes a resident acting company, performing apprentices, and ninety professionals who work with more than three hundred technicians and adult and student actors. Among those working behind the scenes are full-time wig makers, milliners, dye masters, master electricians, seamsters, and draftspersons. And, of course, there is an office staff to handle the administration of the theater and an artistic director to oversee the creative side of the theater. Along with the full-time jobs, there are various part-time jobs.

# The Rewards of Arts and Entertainment Careers

While all children need food, clothing, and shelter, they also need something more—the richness of life that arts and entertainment can offer. Careers in these fields allow you to bring this extra dimension into their lives while giving you a very exciting work life. Not many people are employed in these areas; however, those who are savor the unique pleasure of combining two special loves: the arts or entertainment and working with children.

# More Careers Focusing on Children

*Definition: Kids at heart and others who adore children are
the fortunate individuals who have hundreds of options
in finding careers that let them work with children.*

**E**veryone retains something of the child in the adult. The kid at
heart can build upon the child within by finding a career that
involves being around children and supporting their nurtu-
rance. The purpose of this book is to introduce you to a wide variety of jobs that let you spend your working hours with children.
There are still more careers than have been mentioned in this
book that are excellent choices for those who adore children.
Wherever children are found, there will be jobs that let you deal
with them in some way. So keep your eyes open, and you will discover them.

And, of course, you can also expand your list of jobs dealing
with children by looking at want ads, visiting placement offices at
schools, looking at job listings at state and federal employment
information offices, visiting private employment agencies, brows-
ing through career books, and surfing online. Furthermore, here
are a few more careers that kids at heart and others who adore
children should explore.

# Children's Librarians

Children's librarians work directly with children, helping them find the information that they need. They introduce children to different forms of literature by setting up and conducting children's reading programs. Children's librarians organize reading clubs and storytelling times for children. They familiarize themselves with new books so they can order books for the library that children will enjoy. Also, librarians create book lists for children who wish to explore specific topics such as Indians of North America or the Civil War. Within their world of books and periodicals, children's librarians spend their working days dealing closely with children or performing tasks related to enhancing children's interests in library materials and reading.

Children's librarians work in public libraries, school libraries, and media centers. In order to be a librarian, a master's degree in library science (M.L.S.) is necessary for most public libraries and in some school libraries. In addition, school librarians may need to hold teaching credentials. Some M.L.S. programs take a year to complete, while others take two years. Graduates of M.L.S. programs can look forward to favorable job prospects because of the declining number of such graduates in the 1980s. The employment of librarians will grow about as fast as the average of all occupations through the year 2012.

Earnings vary with the librarian's qualifications and the type, size, and location of the library. Overall, the average income of librarians is more than $43,000 per year. Elementary school librarians, however, average a slightly higher income of more than $45,000.

In many libraries, library assistants are taking on more and more of the traditional jobs of the librarian. Here is another opportunity to work with children in both full-time and part-time positions. There is also the possibility of promotion to supervisory positions.

## What It's Like Bringing Books to Children

While working as a clerk and a library assistant, Celeste Steward soon realized that the route to climbing the career ladder in a library was to obtain her master's degree in library science. Now she is the youth services librarian in a public library in a suburban community. According to Celeste, who chose this job because she wanted to work with children, the best part of her work is doing story time, which lets her bring books alive to her young listeners. Besides organizing and presenting story time, she is responsible for developing the library collection, creating programs, initiating outreach services to get more children to come to the library, and supervising paraprofessional staff as well as library volunteers.

Celeste has found that children's librarians need to know a little about a lot of things not only to answer their young readers' questions but also to update the collection appropriately. She points out that this is not a job for a quiet, introverted person but instead a job for someone who enjoys interacting with people. In summing up her career, this librarian who clearly adores children says, "How could you not want to work with children? They are so eager to learn."

## Children's Photographers

Maneuver a puppet so a child will suddenly smile or display a bewitching grin, then snap that child's picture to capture the moment. A children's photographer must be able to inspire the moment as well as master the technical skill of the picture-taking process. With creative application of the technical aspects of light, lens, film, filters, and camera settings, children's photographers produce pictures of children that their parents cannot resist buying.

Children's photographers may work in commercial studios or be small-business owners. They might work in a private studio, or they may travel to homes, malls, and other settings to take pictures of individual children or groups of children engaged in a particular activity such as sports or music. Also, there are school photographers who go from school to school taking individual and group portraits of children.

Employment of photographers is expected to grow as fast as the average for all occupations through the year 2012. Photography, however, is a very competitive field. Only those who are very skilled or have excellent business skills are able to find salaried jobs or attract enough work to support themselves as self-employed photographers. Salaried photographers who work full-time average more than $24,000 a year. Some very popular photographers earn about $50,000 a year. Although some self-employed photographers earn more, most do not.

There is no one best way to become a children's photographer. Learning on the job is a good approach for portrait photography. There are also approximately one thousand colleges, universities, community and junior colleges, vocational-technical institutes, and private trade and technical schools that offer courses in photography. Basic photography courses cover equipment, processes, and techniques. Children's photographers need good eyesight, artistic ability, and manual dexterity. They also must have the patience to work with children.

## Careers in Children's Museums

In major metropolitan areas, you can usually find museums that are designed just for children. Within the museum are jobs for archivists, curators, administrators, and their assistants. Archivists describe and organize the museum's collection so that individual items can be located easily. Curators oversee the museum's collections and acquire items through purchases, gifts, field exploration, and intermuseum loans. They also plan and prepare exhibits.

Employment as an archivist or curator generally requires graduate training and substantial practical or work experience. Furthermore, competition for jobs as archivists and curators is keen, as there are only a few openings in this field each year. For kids at heart, jobs in museums can be especially enjoyable, as part of the daily work may involve purchasing, cataloging, or setting up a display of trains or dolls while children ride nearby on the museum's classic carousel.

## Youth Ministers

Churches of all faiths offer programs for youth. At larger congregations, there are frequently ministers who work solely with children and teenagers. These youth ministers typically organize and manage centers where young people can get together, start clubs for different age groups, take part in social and religious activities with young people, and do some counseling. They rarely work the traditional nine to five as they must be available to work with children when they are not in school. Some evening work is essential.

The demand for youth ministers is high in areas that have large populations of young people. Most youth ministers hold bachelor's degrees in such areas as social work, education, and counseling. They also should complete course work in theology and psychology. In some congregations, youth ministers are ordained ministers, priests, or rabbis.

## Authors, Illustrators, and Publishers

Generations of children have been enthralled by *Goldilocks and the Three Bears*, *Winnie the Pooh*, and *Alice's Adventures in Wonderland*. They have chanted the lines of Dr. Seuss's many rhyming tales and closely followed the adventures of Charlie in Willy Wonka's chocolate factory. While producing children's books does not allow you to work closely with children, it certainly permits you to contribute greatly to the joy children take in listening to and reading books designed especially for them.

The author creates the book by writing the prose, and the illustrator helps the story come alive by drawing the characters and settings. We all know how menacing the big bad wolf appears, how sweet Little Red Riding Hood looks, and how threatening the woods seem. The editor brings the author and illustrator together, checks that the story is just right for children, and oversees the publishing of the book. Finally, bookstores and libraries make the books available for children. Any one of these jobs lets you share your love of books with children.

## Children's Magazines

All children thrill to receiving mail, especially magazines. Children's magazines offer the same career opportunities as children's books do, including editorial, writing, and illustration jobs. Within this field, the pressure of deadlines must be faced each month, but every month brings the satisfaction every month of having created a product children will enjoy. Some popular children's magazines that offer career opportunities include:

> *Cricket*
> *Highlights*
> *Ladybug*
> *National Geographic Kids*
> *Ranger Rick*
> *Sports Illustrated for Kids*
> *Your Big Backyard*

## Children's Retail Stores

Millions of dollars are spent each day on children's clothing, shoes, and toys. Many specialty stores concentrate solely on selling products that will be used by children. Furthermore, larger stores also have entire departments devoted to the sale of products for children. All these stores have jobs for salespeople that let them deal with children and their parents. A large part of this job involves helping children find the desired jackets, jeans, and shoes. Kids at heart can also have fun demonstrating products such as toys and train sets.

No formal education is required for most jobs selling children's products. Employers do look for people who enjoy working with children and who will be patient in dealing with them. Employment of retail sales workers is expected to grow about as fast as the average for all occupations through the year 2012. Many sales openings will occur because a large number of these workers transfer to other occupations or leave the workforce. Many of the jobs in retail sales are part-time jobs that pay only minimum wage.

## Children's Restaurants

In recent years, a new workplace has emerged for those who want to have a job that lets them be with children. There are now restaurants that focus on children by providing the food and entertainment that children love. Many families hold birthday parties for their children in these restaurants, while others just enjoy the relaxing, child-appropriate atmosphere. Entertainment may be live or consist of a variety of games, from video games to skill games such as making baskets or throwing a ball and hitting a target. Within these restaurants, there are typical restaurant jobs as well as the opportunity to work on the entertainment side of the business.

## Still More Careers

If you find that the more traditional careers described in this book don't appeal to you but you still want to work with children, use your imagination to discover the perfect job. Think of the places where children commonly congregate and what services they need at those spots. This could lead you to become Santa Claus at Christmastime at the mall. Or you could become a decorator specializing in the design of children's rooms or someone who makes homes child safe by installing cabinet locks, window guards, or electrical outlet safety devices. There may be a special skill that you possess that could lead to your establishing an etiquette or computer school for children.

Besides careers working directly with children, a great number of jobs involve doing things that benefit, educate, or entertain children. In this category, you will find the inventor who designs safer playground equipment or a better bicycle helmet. You will also find the researcher who discovers a cure for childhood leukemia or liver disorders.

Fashion designers create imaginative yet sturdy clothing for children. And others create innovative children's puzzles or computer games. For those who adore children, spending one's life working in a career that will benefit children in some way or bring more laughter into their lives can be immensely rewarding.

## An Overview of Job Opportunities

An immense variety of jobs exists that will permit kids at heart to spend their workdays with their favorite people—children. The fastest-growing job market is in the area of child care. More jobs than ever before exist for those who want to care for children in their own homes, others' homes, and child care centers. A very large number of jobs also exists for those who wish to teach children, whether it is in preschools, elementary schools, middle schools, or high schools. And teaching children is not confined to the traditional schoolhouse—many jobs are available to instruct children in sports, music, art, dance, and other skills. Working as a health care professional must be very satisfying to those who adore children because such professionals play a major role in keeping children healthy. Careers in child welfare and juvenile justice permit those who care about children to make a significant difference in children's lives. Kids at heart can also look forward to careers entertaining children and showing them how to enjoy recreational activities.

With so many opportunities to be found, the future is bright for job-seeking kids at heart and others who adore children.

# Professional Organizations

One way to learn more about careers for kids at heart and others who adore children is by contacting organizations associated with these careers. You can also visit many of these organizations online. This section lists organizations for each chapter of the book.

## Child Care Center Careers

For information on careers in educating young children, contact:

National Association for the Education of Young Children
1509 Sixteenth Street NW
Washington, DC 20036
www.naeyc.org

For eligibility requirements and a description of the Child Development Associate credential, contact:

Council for Early Childhood Professions Recognition
2460 Sixteenth Street NW
Washington, DC 20009
www.cdacouncil.org

For information on child care work, contact:

National Child Care Information Center
10530 Rosehaven Street, Suite 400
Fairfax, VA 22103
www.nccic.org

For information on opportunities in AmeriCorps, contact:

AmeriCorps
1201 New York Avenue
Washington, DC 20525
www.americorps.org

## At-Home Child Care Careers

For information on careers in home child care, contact:

National Association of Child Care Resource & Referral
    Agencies
3101 Wilson Boulevard, Suite 350
Arlington, VA 22201
www.naccrra.net

For information on becoming a family child care provider, contact the National Child Care Information Center listed above or
the following:

Children's Foundation
725 Fifteenth Street NW, Suite 505
Washington, DC 20005
www.childrensfoundation.net

# Nanny Careers

For information on becoming a professional nanny, contact:

International Nanny Association
2020 Southwest Freeway, Suite 208
Houston, TX 77098
www.nanny.org

# Babysitting Careers

You can obtain information about babysitter training from:

American Red Cross National Headquarters
2025 E Street NW
Washington, DC 20006
www.redcross.org

# Teaching Careers

For additional information on accredited teacher education programs, contact:

National Council for Accreditation of Teacher Education
2010 Massachusetts Avenue NW, Suite 500
Washington, DC 20036
www.ncate.org

Council for Professional Recognition
2460 Sixteenth Street NW
Washington, DC 20009
www.cdacouncil.org

For information on teachers' unions and education-related issues, contact:

American Federation of Teachers
555 New Jersey Avenue NW
Washington, DC 20001
www.aft.org

National Education Association
1201 Sixteenth Street NW
Washington, DC 20036
www.nea.org

For information on the teaching profession and on how to become a teacher, contact:

Recruiting New Teachers
385 Concord Avenue, Suite 103
Belmont, MA 02478
www.rnt.org

## Sports and Recreation Careers

For information on sports careers, contact:

National Association for Sport and Physical Education
American Alliance for Health, Physical Education, Recreation, & Dance
1900 Association Drive
Reston, VA 22091
www.aahperd.org/naspe

National Alliance for Youth Sports
2050 Vista Parkway
West Palm Beach, FL 33411
www.nays.org

For information on recreation careers, contact:

American Camping Association
5000 State Road 67 North
Martinsville, IN 46151
www.acacamps.org

National Recreation and Park Association
22377 Belmont Ridge Road
Ashburn, VA 20148
www.nrpa.org

## Children's Health Careers

For information on dentistry as a career and a list of accredited dental schools, contact:

American Academy of Pediatric Dentistry
211 East Chicago Avenue
Chicago, IL 60611
www.ada.org

American Dental Education Association
1400 K NW, Suite 1100
Washington, DC 20005
www.adea.org

American Dental Hygienists' Association
Division of Education
444 North Michigan Avenue, Suite 3400
Chicago, IL 60611
www.adha.org

For information on pediatric care careers, contact:

American Academy of Pediatrics
141 Northwest Point Boulevard
Elk Grove Village, IL 60007
www.aap.org

American Medical Association
Department of Communications and Public Relations
515 North State Street
Chicago, IL 60610
www.ama-assn.org

American Nurses Association
8515 Georgia Avenue, Suite 400
Silver Spring, MD 20910
www.nursingworld.org

American Association of Colleges of Nursing
One Dupont Circle NW, Suite 530
Washington, DC 20036
www.aacn.nche.edu

National League for Nursing
61 Broadway
New York, NY 10006
www.nln.org

For information on psychology careers, contact:

National Association of School Psychologists
4340 East West Highway, Suite 402
Bethesda, MD 20814
www.nasponline.org

American Psychological Association
750 First Street NE
Washington, DC 20002
www.apa.org

For information on psychiatry careers, contact:

American Psychiatric Association
1000 Wilson Boulevard, Suite 1825
Arlington, VA 22209
www.psych.org

# Child Welfare Careers

To obtain information on careers in social work, contact:

Council on Social Work Education
1725 Duke Street, Suite 500
Alexandria, VA 22314
www.cswe.org

National Association of Social Workers
Career Information
750 First Street NE, Suite 700
Washington, DC 20002
www.socialworkers.org

For information on juvenile justice careers, contact:

National Court Appointed Special Advocate Association
100 West Harrison Street, North Tower, Suite 500
Seattle, WA 98119
www.nationalcasa.org

National Council of Juvenile and Family Court Judges
University of Nevada
PO Box 8970
Reno, NV 89507
www.ncjfcj.org

# Arts and Entertainment Careers

For careers in the arts, contact:

American Dance Guild
PO Box 2006, Lenox Hill Station
New York, NY 10021
www.americandanceguild.org

Dance Educators of America
PO Box 607
Pelham, NY 10803
www.deadance.com

National Association of Schools of Dance
11250 Roger Bacon Drive, Suite 21
Reston, VA 20190
http://nasd.arts-accredit.org

National Dance Council of America
PO Box 22018
Provo, UT 84602
www.ndca.org

National Association for Music Education
1806 Robert Fulton Drive
Reston, VA 20191
www.menc.org

National Art Education Association
1916 Association Drive
Reston, VA 20191
www.naea-reston.org

Professional Photographers of America
229 Peachtree Street NE, Suite 2200
Atlanta, GA 30303
www.ppa.com

For careers in entertainment, contact:

Clowns of America, International
PO Box C
Richeyville, PA 15358
www.clownsofamerica.org

International Brotherhood of Magicians
11155 South Towne Square, Suite C
St. Louis, MO 63123
www.magician.org

# More Careers Focusing on Children

For additional information on careers working with children, contact:

Association for Library Service to Children
American Library Association
50 East Huron Street
Chicago, IL 60611
www.ala.org/ala/alsc

Association of Children's Museums
1300 L Street NW, Suite 975
Washington, DC 20005
www.childrensmuseums.org

Society of Children's Book Writers & Illustrators
8271 Beverly Boulevard
Los Angeles, CA 90048
www.scbwi.org

# About the Authors

M arjorie Eberts and Margaret Gisler have been writing together professionally for twenty-five years. They are prolific freelance authors with more than eighty books in print, including twenty-one career books. Much of their writing is in the field of education. The two authors have written textbooks, beginning readers, and study skills books for schoolchildren and developed supplementary reading programs for the elementary level. They have also written a book on preparing children for kindergarten and a college preparation handbook.

Besides writing books, the two authors write a King Features syndicated education column, "Dear Teacher," which appears in newspapers throughout the country. Their column gives parents advice on how to guide their children successfully through school. Eberts and Gisler also give advice on education issues in speeches, at workshops, and on television.

Writing this book was a special pleasure for the authors as it gave them the opportunity to meet so many caring people who are guaranteeing that the next generation of children will be a great one. Since they are also the parents of six children between them, they doubly appreciate the efforts of all those involved in the care of children.

Eberts is a graduate of Stanford University, and Gisler is a graduate of Ball State University and Butler University. Both received their specialist degrees in education from Butler University, and Gisler is currently completing a doctorate in education at Ball State. The two authors are also teachers with a combined experience of more than twenty years of teaching.